OUTLINE OF HANDBOOK

ENGLISH HANDBOOK

ENGLISH HANDBOOK

FLOYD C. WATKINS

WILLIAM B. DILLINGHAM

HOUGHTON MIFFLIN COMPANY · BOSTON

Atlanta   Dallas   Geneva, Illinois
Hopewell, New Jersey   Palo Alto   Toronto

Floyd C. Watkins and William B. Dillingham are
Professors of English at Emory University, Atlanta.

Library of Congress Catalog Card Number: 78-58859

Student's Edition ISBN: 0-395-26720-X

Teacher's Edition ISBN: 0-395-26721-8

Acknowledgments

Acknowledgment is made to the following sources of reprinted materials.

Abridged and adapted from pp. 1–2 in *Titans of the Seas,* by James H. Belote and William M. Belote. Copyright © 1975 by James H. Belote and William M. Belote. Used by permission of Harper & Row, Publishers, Inc.

From Rachel Carson, *The Sea Around Us,* Copyright 1950, 1951 by Rachel L. Carson. Copyright © renewed 1961 by Rachel L. Carson. Copyright © renewed 1978, 1979 by Roger Christie. Reprinted by permission of the Estate of the Author, and Oxford University Press, Inc.

From Carlos Clarens, *An Illustrated History of the Horror Films.* New York: G. P. Putnam's Sons, 1967.

From Maisie and Robert Conrat, "How U.S. farmers became specialists—in cash and debts," *The American Farm.* Copyright © 1977 by Maisie Conrat and Robert Conrat. Reprinted by permission of Houghton Mifflin Company.

From Alexander DeConde, *Half Bitter, Half Sweet: An Excursion into Italian-American History.* Copyright © 1971 by Alexander DeConde. Reprinted with the permission of Charles Scribner's Sons.

From Philip Durham and Everett L. Jones, *The Frontier in American Literature.* Copyright © 1969 by The Bobbs-Merrill Co., Inc. Reprinted by permission of The Bobbs-Merrill Co.

From James K. Feibleman, *The Stages of Human Life: A Biography of Entire Man.* Atlantic Highlands, N.J.: Humanities Press, 1976.

From pp. 4–5 (from *vie* to *loll*) and pp. 35–37 (*semantics* to *mawkish*) (in the Bantam edition) of *It Pays to Increase Your Word Power,* by Peter Funk (Funk & Wagnalls). Copyright © 1969 by Peter V. K. Funk. Used by permission of Harper & Row, Publishers, Inc.

From Ira J. Gordon, *Human Development: From Birth to Adolescence,* 2nd ed. New York: Harper and Row, 1969.

Adapted from Felix Guirand, "Greek Mythology," *New Larousse Enclyclopedia of Mythology.* London: The Hamlyn Publishing Group Ltd. © 1959 Paul Hamlyn.

From Gilbert Highet, *The Art of Teaching.* Copyright 1950 by Gilbert Highet. Reprinted by permission of Alfred A. Knopf, Inc.

From Edmund S. Morgan, "George Washington: The Aloof American," *The Meaning of Independence.* Copyright 1976. Reprinted by permission of The University Press of Virginia.

From Elizabeth Nitchie, *Mary Shelley: Author of "Frankenstein."* New Brunswick, N.J.: Rutgers University Press, 1953.

Contents

ENGLISH
HANDBOOK

Sentence Errors and Grammar

1 Sentence Fragments

Do not use meaningless or ineffective fragments.

A **fragment** is a part of a sentence written and punctuated as a complete sentence. It is harder to recognize in a group of several sentences than it is when it is written separately. It may be a dependent clause (group of words that contains a subject and a verb but is not able to stand alone as a sentence), a phrase, or any other word group which violates the accepted subject-verb sentence pattern. Fragments may reflect incomplete or confused thinking.

Fragment   That she had heard all the trite comments about the weather which she could endure in one day. *(Dependent noun clause)*

Complete   She had heard all the trite comments about the weath-
Sentence   er which she could endure in one day.

Fragment   The poem which refers to fish that have one fin cut off to show that they are stocked by the government. *(Noun plus dependent clause)*

1

Complete Sentence The poem refers to fish that have one fin cut off to show that they are stocked by the government.

Fragment Although some students are well trained in the techniques used by high school debaters. *(Dependent adverbial clause)*

Complete Sentence Some students are well trained in the techniques used by high school debaters.

Fragment The dense forest humming with sounds of insects and teeming with animal life. *(Noun plus participial phrases)*

Complete Sentence The dense forest hummed with sounds of insects and teemed with animal life.

Fragment The color of neon lights reflected in the rain, the greenery of parks amid concrete, the sparkling glass of new buildings. *(Nouns and phrases)*

Complete Sentence A city offers much beauty: the color of neon lights reflected in the rain, the greenery of parks amid concrete, the sparkling glass of new buildings.

Fragments are often permissible in dialogue when the meaning is clear from the context.

"See the geese."
"Where?"
"Flying north."

Sometimes fragments create special effects or emphasis.

It is one of the loveliest of stories. *So much irony; so much humour; so kind and understanding; and wrapped up in the most delicate poetic mood.* SEAN O'FAOLAIN, *The Short Story*

This long fragment lacks subject and verb ("It has" or "It contains"), but the careful parallelism of the elements set off by semicolons indicates skill—not ignorance or carelessness.

1

● *Exercise 1*

Decide how the following fragments could be made into complete sentences by omitting, adding, or changing only one word.

1. The guest speaker addressing the graduating seniors, the principal, and members of the audience.

2. That the time will come when the last bald eagle has flown high over the mountain tops looking for prey.

3. Rivers with poisonous chemicals from factories, garbage dumped by cities and towns, and various other ugly products of civilization.

4. Because a difficult educational situation occurs when the learner simply does not have the background to understand the problem that must be solved.

5. There in the desert a mirage of cool water running over rocks.

6. Since she was well acquainted with my family.

7. Outside the courtroom a crowd gathering.

8. The lithographic portraits and biographical sketches of nineteenth-century Native American men and women revealing much of historical importance.

9. The pictures which were on display at the Smithsonian.

10. That the world-famous airport lay on the other side of the city.

2

2 Comma Splices and Fused Sentences

Use a semicolon or a comma and a coordinating conjunction *(and, but, or, nor, for, yet, so)* to join two independent clauses (clauses that could stand alone as sentences).

A **comma splice,** or comma fault, occurs when independent clauses have a comma but no coordinating conjunction between them.

In a **fused sentence,** or run-on sentence, the independent clauses have neither punctuation nor a coordinating conjunction between them.

Comma splices and fused sentences fail to indicate the strong break between independent clauses. They may be corrected in four principal ways:

1. Use a *period* and write two sentences.
2. Use a *semicolon.*
3. Use a *comma* and a *coordinating conjunction.*
4. Make one of the clauses *dependent.*

See also **23.**

Splice   Human nature is seldom as simple as it appears, hasty judgments are therefore often wrong.

Fused   Human nature is seldom as simple as it appears hasty judgments are therefore often wrong.

Corrections   1. Human nature is seldom as simple as it appears. Hasty judgments are therefore often wrong.
2. Human nature is seldom as simple as it appears; hasty judgments are therefore often wrong.
3. Human nature is seldom as simple as it appears, and hasty judgments are therefore often wrong.
4. Because human nature is seldom as simple as it appears, hasty judgments are often wrong.

When possible, subordinate one clause (that is, make it a dependent clause) or reduce it to a phrase or even a single word.

In (4) one of the independent clauses is made a dependent adverbial clause. The sentence might also be rewritten as follows:

Clause Human nature is *so* complex *that hasty judgments are often wrong.*

or

Phrase Hasty judgments often overlook *the complexities of human nature.*

Before conjunctive adverbs (*however, moreover, therefore, furthermore,* and so on) use a semicolon to join independent clauses.

> The rare book had a torn flyleaf; therefore it was advertised at a reduced price.

• *Exercise 2*

Identify the comma splices and fused sentences, and decide how they might best be corrected. Note: one sentence is correct as written.

1. Television sometimes offers worthwhile shows as well as trivia, it should not be condemned uncritically.
2. After twelve years of silence the great composer finished two brilliant symphonies within six months.
3. Conflicts almost always exist within a family however, it is still the most enduring of social units.
4. One ancient culture practiced the art of carving masks another expressed itself creatively in weaving elaborate tapestries.

5. A famous rose enthusiast wrote that it is necessary to love roses in order to cultivate them successfully growers must have roses in their hearts if they are to have them in their gardens.

- ## Exercise 3

Decide how the following fragments, comma splices, and fused sentences might be made into correct sentences. Note: some sentences are correct as written.

1. Economy is a virtue up to a point, beyond that it may become a vice.
2. Destroyers uproot trees and move vast quantities of earth but do not replace the soil.
3. Young people have always created their own varieties of music growing older, they reject the music that comes after their youth.
4. In case of fire people should never lose their heads, on the contrary, they should think clearly and act deliberately.
5. New York's Washington Square has changed considerably since it was a haven for writers in the 1890's.
6. In a lonely village on the seacoast, where the primitive beauty of nature still survives.
7. The Great Depression of the 1930's caused much unhappiness in some families, others it brought closer together.

8. Earth may be the only planet. Which will support human life.

9. If humanity is to prosper, therefore, the natural environment must be preserved.

10. An adventurer will sometimes participate in a pastime despite great danger, skydiving, for example, is perilous.

• *Exercise 4*

Decide how the following fragments, comma splices, and fused sentences might be made into correct sentences. Note: some sentences are correct as written.

1. In some parts of the world practical matters take precedence over love, marriages are still arranged by parents.

2. Some generous people are naive, they simply do not realize when they are being imposed upon.

3. Some say that nonconformity for its own sake. Has become a fad.

4. The students had never before studied the mechanics of composition.

5. Science and art are not incompatible, some learned scientists are also philosophers or poets.

6. The art of pleasing is a very necessary talent. But a very difficult one to acquire.

3

7. Kindness can hardly be reduced to rules good will and thoughtfulness will lead to congenial relationships with others.

8. "Do as you would be done by" is the surest method of pleasing.

9. Clothes inappropriate to a place or situation are absurd a mink coat on a beach in July would be comical.

10. Many people think of earthquakes as occurring only in the West actually, earthquakes occur in other parts of the country as well.

3 Verb Forms
Use the correct form of the verb.

All verbs have three **principal parts:** the present infinitive *(to work),* the past tense *(worked),* and the past participle *(worked).* The past participle is used with an **auxiliary,** or helping, **verb,** as in the sentence "She had worked in the store for three months." Verbs are regular or irregular in their principal parts.

Regular verbs *(help, talk, nail, open, close)* form the past tense and the past participle by adding *-d* or *-ed* or sometimes *-t* (as in *burnt, dwelt*). Thus the principal parts of *to close* are *close, closed, closed;* those of *to talk* are *talk, talked, talked.*

Irregular verbs usually form the past tense and the past participle by changing an internal vowel: *drink, drank, drunk.* Consult a dictionary when in doubt. For an irregular verb like *think,* the dictionary also gives *thought* (the form of the past tense and the past participle) and *thinking* (the present participle). It may also give the present tense form *thinks.* The principal parts are *think, thought, thought.* You should know the following troublesome verbs so well that you automatically use them correctly.

Infinitive	Past Tense	Past Participle
awake	awoke, awaked	awaked, awoke
be	was	been
begin	began	begun
bid (to offer as a price or to make a bid in playing cards)	bid	bid
bid (to command, order)	bade	bidden, bid
blow	blew	blown
bring	brought	brought
build	built	built
burst	burst	burst
choose	chose	chosen
come	came	come
deal	dealt	dealt
dig	dug	dug
dive	dived, dove	dived
do	did	done
drag	dragged	dragged
draw	drew	drawn
drink	drank	drunk
drive	drove	driven
drown	drowned	drowned
fly	flew	flown
freeze	froze	frozen
give	gave	given
go	went	gone
grow	grew	grown
hang (to execute)	hanged	hanged
hang (to suspend)	hung	hung

Infinitive	Past Tense	Past Participle
know	knew	known
lead	led	led
lend	lent	lent
lose	lost	lost
ring	rang	rung
run	ran	run
see	saw	seen
shine (to give light)	shone	shone
shine (to polish)	shined	shined
sing	sang, sung	sung
sink	sank, sunk	sunk
sting	stung	stung
swim	swam	swum
swing	swung	swung
take	took	taken
teach	taught	taught
throw	threw	thrown
wear	wore	worn
write	wrote	written

In a few confusing pairs of verbs it helps to remember that one is **transitive** (may take an object) and that the other is **intransitive** (does not take an object):

Transitive	lay (to place)	laid	laid
Intransitive	lie (to recline)	lay	lain
Transitive	set (to place in position)	set	set
Intransitive	sit (to be seated)	sat	sat
Transitive	raise (to lift)	raised	raised
Intransitive	rise (to get up)	rose	risen

Set also has intransitive forms: a hen *sets;* concrete *sets;* the sun *sets.*

• *Exercise 5*

Identify the incorrect verbs below and decide on the correct forms. Note: some verb forms are correct as written.

1. She always laid down for a nap on Sunday afternoons.

2. The rain begun during the night.

3. My grandparents come to stay with us for a week.

4. The thirsty animal drunk a whole bowl of water.

5. He give me a reward for finding his watch.

6. The lone figure set on the bench long after the departure of the bus.

7. On New Year's Eve the church bells were rung at midnight.

8. At the ball park the crowd had rose to sing the national anthem.

9. She swum the backstroke faster than anyone else at the meet.

10. He had never worn a tuxedo before.

4 Tense and Sequence of Tenses

Use verbs to express distinctions in time. Avoid unnecessary shifts in tense.

For each of the three kinds of time—present, past, and future—verbs have different tense forms: simple, progressive, and perfect.

	Irregular	**Regular**
Simple		
Present	I go	I walk
Past	I went	I walked
Future	I shall (will) go	I shall (will) walk
Progressive		
Present	I am going	I am walking
Past	I was going	I was walking
Future	I shall (will) be going	I shall (will) be walking
Perfect		
Present	I have gone	I have walked
Past	I had gone	I had walked
Future	I shall (will) have gone	I shall (will) have walked

In general, the **present tense** expresses present time, but there are exceptions. Compare the following:

I *eat* lunch. (simple present tense—with the force of repeated action)

I *am eating* lunch. (present progressive tense—present action)

I *leave* for New York tomorrow. (present tense—future action)

I *am leaving* in fifteen minutes. (present progressive tense—future action)

As the last two examples illustrate, the time expressed by the tense form is often determined by a word or a phrase.

Statements about the contents of literature and other works of art generally take the present tense (historical present).

In Henry James's *The Turn of the Screw* a governess *believes* that she sees ghosts.

Statements of natural truth or scientific law also take the present tense regardless of the controlling verb.

In 1851 Foucault proved that the earth *rotates* on its axis.

But Ancient Greeks *believed* that the earth *was* motionless.

The three **perfect tenses** indicate time or action completed before another time or action.

Present Perfect with Present
I *have bought* my ticket, and I **am waiting** for the bus.

The controlling time word need not be a verb.

I *have bought* my ticket **already.**

Past Perfect with Past
I *had bought* my ticket, and I **was waiting** for the bus.
I *had bought* my ticket before the bus **came.**

Future Perfect with Future
I *shall have eaten* by the time we **go.** (The controlling word, *go,* is present tense in form but future in meaning.)

I *shall have eaten* by **one o'clock.**

The future perfect is rare. Usually the simple future tense is used with an adverbial phrase or clause.

Rare I shall have eaten before I go.
More Common I shall eat before I go.

In dialogue the present tense is often used for the future.

"When are you leaving?"
"We leave at dawn."

Relationships between verbs should be logical and consistent:

Two Past Actions
The sailor *stood* on the shore and *threw* pebbles at the seagulls. (Not *throws*)

He *turned* away when he *saw* me watching him.

Two Present Actions
As the school year *draws* to a close, the students *are swept* into a whirl of activities.

Future Actions

Some *will go* to the sea for their vacations, some *will go* to the desert, but few *will go* to the city.

An infinitive (see **49**) generally takes the present tense when it expresses action which occurs at the same time as that of the controlling verb.

Not   I wanted *to have gone.*
But   I wanted *to go.*

Not   I had expected *to have met* my friends at the game.
But   I had expected *to meet* my friends at the game.

Not   I would have preferred *to have waited* until they came.
But   I would have preferred *to wait* until they came.

The perfect participle expresses an action which precedes another action.

Having finished the novel, the elderly author stored it in her safe with the others.

● *Exercise 6*

Identify the incorrect verbs and decide on the correct forms. Note: one sentence is correct as written.

1. In looking back, public officials almost always say that they would have preferred to have remained private citizens.

2. The actor opened the Bible and begins reading from the Book of Psalms.

3. It was Goethe's feeling that genius was simply "consummate industry."

4. She boards the plane as soon as the flight was announced.

5. She had hoped to have gotten a scholarship to the university.

6. After having laid on the bottom of the bay for centuries, the Swedish ship was risen and placed in a museum.

7. Hundreds of dusty arrowheads and spearpoints were laying on the shelves in the study.

8. After it sets, concrete is a durable material for roads.

9. Joseph Conrad was well into his thirties before he begun to write his novels.

10. After the *Titanic* had sank, the world at first found the tragedy difficult to believe.

5 Voice

Use the active voice except when the context demands the passive.

A transitive verb is either active or passive. When the subject acts, the verb is active. When the subject is acted upon, the verb is passive. In most sentences the actor is more important than the receiver of the action. A weak passive verb may leave the actor unknown or seemingly ineffective.

Weak Passive   The huge iceberg *was rammed* into by the luxury liner.
Strong Active   The luxury liner *rammed* into the huge iceberg.

Weak Passive   A good race *was run* by the Ferrari.
Strong Active   The Ferrari *ran* a good race.

5

The active voice helps to create a more concise and vigorous style. The passive voice, however, is sometimes useful when the performer of an action is irrelevant or unimportant:

> The book about motorcycles *had been misplaced* among books about cosmetics.

The passive voice can also be effective when the emphasis is on the receiver, the verb, or even a modifier:

> The police *were* totally *misled.*

• Exercise 7

Decide whether the verb in each of the following sentences is active or passive.

1. Jazz has been called the only original American art form.
2. The new group played at the club party last night.
3. She has become the city's leading bassoonist.
4. The chorus sang two short encores.
5. The theater was filled for the rock concert.

• Exercise 8

Decide in which sentences the verb is effective. When the verb is not effective, decide how to improve it by changing the voice.

1. The bird's nest was flown into directly by the mother bird, which brought a worm to feed her young.

2. Some young people are learning the almost-lost art of shoeing horses.

3. The horse lost the race because the shoe had been improperly nailed to the hoof.

4. Sharp curves are not well negotiated by many people just learning to drive.

5. The rare plants were not properly cared for by the gardener.

6 Subjunctive Mood

In using the subjunctive mood, be guided by idiom.

The subjunctive in English has been traditionally employed to express commands, requests, wishes, and conditions which are improbable or contrary to fact. Today the subjunctive survives largely as a matter of idiom—of natural speech forms. In sentences like "I wouldn't do that if I *were* you," the choice of the subjunctive is natural. Although a member of an organization still says, "I move that the meeting *be* adjourned," he or she is actually using a phrase which has frozen into the language. Some old subjunctives with *be* have disappeared ("If I *be* right, that is a rare coin"). Occasionally "If this be true" is heard—but not often.

7 Subject and Verb: Agreement

Use singular verbs with singular subjects, plural verbs with plural subjects.

The *-s* or *-es* ending of the third person present tense (he talks, she wishes) of the *verb* indicates the **singular;** the -s or -es ending of a *noun* indicates the **plural.**

Singular   The dog barks. The ax cuts. The ax does cut.
Plural   The dogs bark. The axes cut. The axes do cut.

7a   A compound subject with *and* takes a plural verb.

Two or more subjects connected by a coordinating conjunction, such as *and,* are said to be compound.

Work and *play* **are** not equally rewarding.

Baseball and *swimming* **are** usually summer sports.

Exception: Compound subjects connected by *and* but expressing a singular idea may take a singular verb.

Bacon and eggs **is** my favorite breakfast.

Your *name and address* **is** sufficient.

7b   After a compound subject with *or, nor, either . . . or, neither . . . nor, not . . . but*, the verb agrees with the nearer part of the subject.

Neither the *consumer* nor the *producer* **is** pleased by higher taxes.

Either *fans* or an *air conditioner* **is** necessary.

Either an *air conditioner* or *fans* **are** necessary.

Neither *you* nor your *successor* **is** affected by the new regulation.

In informal speech a plural verb may be used to express a plural with *neither . . . nor.*

Neither *television* nor the *press* **are** unduly censored.

7c Intervening phrases or clauses not introduced by coordinating conjunctions do not affect the number of a verb.

Connectives like *as well as* and *along with* are not coordinating conjunctions but prepositions; they do not form compound subjects. Other such words and phrases include *in addition to, together with, with, plus,* and *including.*

The *engine* as well as the wings **was** destroyed in the crash.

The *pilot* along with all his passengers **was** rescued.

7d A collective noun takes a singular verb when referring to a group as a unit, a plural verb when the members of a group are thought of individually.

A collective noun names a class or group: *family, flock, jury, audience,* and so on.

My *family* **is** going on vacation soon.

The *jury* **were** taking their seats in the courtroom.

7e Most nouns plural in form but singular in meaning take a singular verb.

Economics and *news* are considered singular; *trousers* and *scissors* are treated as plural except when used after *pair.* When in doubt, consult a dictionary. *Data* is considered singular or plural; the singular form, *datum,* is rare.

Economics is often thought of as a science.

The *news* of the defeat is disappointing.

Tactics is the art of maneuvering military forces.

British and American military *tactics* were different.

The *trousers* are unpressed and frayed about the cuffs.

An old *pair* of *trousers* is essential for his costume.

The *scissors* are dull.

That *pair* of *scissors* is dull.

7f Indefinite pronouns, such as *each, either, neither, one, no one, everyone, someone, anyone, nobody, everybody, somebody, anybody,* usually take singular verbs.

Neither of his ideas was suitable for a short report.

Everybody has trouble choosing a subject for an essay.

Each student has chosen a subject for a report.

A plural verb with words like *each* is gaining some acceptance in informal speech.

Each of the divers are allowed to follow their individual styles.

7g Some words, such as *none, some, part, all, half* (and other fractions), take a singular or a plural verb, depending on the noun or pronoun which follows.

singular
Some of the sugar **was** spilled on the floor.

plural
Some of the apples **were** spilled on the floor.

singular
Half of the money **is** yours.

plural
Half of the students **are** looking out the window.

None is considered sometimes singular, sometimes plural:

None of those accused **was** really responsible.

None of those accused **were** really responsible.

The number, when used as the subject, is usually singular:

The number of people in the audience **was** never determined.

A number is considered equivalent to the adjective *some,* and the noun or pronoun which follows controls the verb:

A number of the *guests* **were** whispering.

7h In sentences beginning with *There* or *Here* followed by verb and subject, the verb is singular or plural depending on the subject.

There and *Here* are devices **(expletives)** sometimes used when the subject follows the verb.

There **was** a long *interval* between the two discoveries.

There **were** thirteen *blackbirds* perched on the fence.

Here **is** a *thing* to remember.

Here **are** two *things* to remember.

The singular *There is* may be used to introduce a compound subject when the first noun is singular.

There **is** a *swing* and a *footbridge* in the garden.

In sentences beginning with *It,* the verb is singular.

It **was** many years ago.

7i A verb agrees with its subject, not with a subjective complement (word or group of words following a linking verb, such as *be* or *seem,* and identifying the subject).

His *horse* and his *dog* **are** his main source of pleasure.

His main *source* of pleasure **is** his horse and his dog.

7j After a relative pronoun *(who, which, that)* the verb has the same person and number as the antecedent (word to which a pronoun refers).

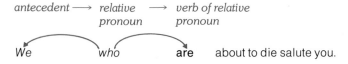

antecedent ⟶ *relative* ⟶ *verb of relative*
pronoun *pronoun*

We *who* **are** about to die salute you.

The *costumes which* **were** worn in the ballet were dazzling.

He was the *candidate who* **was** able to carry out his campaign pledges.

He was one of the *candidates who* **were** able to carry out their campaign pledges.

But He was the only *one* of the candidates *who* **was** able to carry out his campaign pledges.

7k A title is singular and requires a singular verb even if it contains plural words and plural ideas.

The Canterbury Tales **is** a masterpiece of comedy.

• *Exercise 9*

Decide how to correct each verb that does not agree with its subject. Identify the sentences that are correct as written.

1. The sound of hammers mingle with the screech of sea-gulls and the crash of waves on the beach.
2. In O'Neill's *Long Day's Journey into Night,* Mary's smiles and laughter are increasingly forced.
3. D. H. Lawrence's *Sons and Lovers* are a landmark among the novels of the time.
4. A large number of the actors was not audible in the back of the auditorium.
5. The driver together with the two passengers were injured in the accident.
6. Ethics are the study of moral philosophy and standards of conduct.

7. Everyone at the conference has come a long way to attend.

8. This tribal custom is enforced by strict taboos, the violation of which bring immediate death.

9. Rambling sentences or dull writing are not improved by a sprinkling of dashes.

10. Neither money nor power satisfy the deepest human needs of those who seek to fulfill themselves.

• *Exercise 10*

Decide how to correct each verb that does not agree with its subject. Identify the sentences that are correct as written.

1. A vacation of at least two weeks are looked forward to all year long.

2. The family have gone to Hawaii.

3. His job, like that of thousands of others, is threatened by the company's recent decision.

4. There is worse fates than not keeping up with the Joneses.

5. His favorite place to spend a weekend are either the mountains or the beach.

6. You or she are the person to take the minutes of the meeting.

7. Physics are her best school subject.

8. Nobody except the coach and the team members know what happened in the locker room before the game.

9. She is the only one of the witnesses of the accident who are testifying at the trial.

10. Some of the committee members are not planning to attend the conference.

8 Pronouns: Agreement and Reference

Use singular pronouns to refer to singular antecedents, plural pronouns to refer to plural antecedents. Make pronouns refer to a definite antecedent.

She took **her** books.

They took **their** books.

8a In general, use a plural pronoun to refer to a compound antecedent with *and.*

The *owner* and the *captain* refused to leave **their** distressed ship.

If two nouns designate the same person, the pronoun is singular.

The *owner and captain* refused to leave **his** distressed ship.

8b After a compound antecedent with *or, nor, either . . . or, neither . . nor, not only . . . but also,* a pronoun agrees with the nearer part of the antecedent (see **7b**).

Neither the *Secretary* nor the *Undersecretary* was in **his** seat.

> Neither the *Secretary* nor his *aides* were consistent in their policy.

A sentence like this written with *and* is less stilted.

> The Secretary and his aides were not consistent in their policy.

In informal speech a plural pronoun may be used to express a plural with *neither . . . nor.*

> Neither *Nicholas* nor *Alexandra* lost **their** dignity under pressure.

8c A singular pronoun follows a collective noun antecedent when the members of the group are considered as a unit; a plural pronoun, when they are thought of individually (see **7d**).

A Unit The student *committee* presented **its** report.

Individuals The *committee* filed into the room and took **their** seats.

8d Such singular antecedents as *each, either, neither, one, no one, everybody, someone, anyone, nobody, everybody, somebody, anybody* usually call for singular pronouns.

> Not *one* of the football players felt that **he** had played a good game.

> *Everyone* in the Girl Scout troop took **her** sleeping bag on the camping trip.

NOTE When a singular pronoun refers to persons of both sexes (as *his* has been used in the past to refer to a man or a woman), there is now no simple solution: *his* to refer to a person when the sex is not known may raise objections; *his or her* is ungainly and should be used sparingly. The best practice may be to avoid the problem when possible.

Ungainly	Each young rider successfully rode *his or her* horse.
Objectionable to Some	Each young rider successfully rode *his* horse.
Alternate Choice	The young riders successfully rode *their* horses.

The use of a singular pronoun to refer to a single antecedent can sometimes sound stilted. In informal speech it is acceptable to use *they, their,* or *them.*

Everybody cheered. I was pleased to hear *them.*

8e *Which* refers to animals and things. *Who* refers to persons but may be used with animals and some things called by name. *That* refers to animals or things and sometimes to persons.

The *boy* **who** was fishing is my brother.

The *dog* **which (that)** sat beside him looked listless.

Sometimes *that* and *who* are interchangeable.

Children *who (that)* suck their thumbs are often insecure.
A person *who (that)* giggles is often insecure.

NOTE *Whose* (the possessive form of *who*) is often used to avoid the awkward *of which,* even in referring to animals and things.

The *car* **whose** right front tire blew out crashed and burned.

8f Pronouns should not refer vaguely to an entire sentence or clause or to unidentified people.

Many fuzzy references result from starting a sentence without foreseeing problems that will come up.

Confusing   Some people worry about wakefulness but actually need little sleep. *This* is one reason they have so much trouble sleeping.

This could refer to the worry, to the need for little sleep, to psychological problems, or to other traits which have not even been mentioned in the sentence.

Clear   Some people have trouble sleeping because they lie awake and worry about their inability to sleep.

They, them, it, and *you* are sometimes used as vague references to people and conditions which need more precise identification.

Vague   *They* always get *you* in the end.

The problem here is that the pronouns *they* and *you* and the sentence are so vague that the writer could mean almost anything pessimistic. The sentence could be referring to school officials, government officials, or even all of life.

NOTE In informal writing especially, experienced writers sometimes let *this, which,* or *it* refer to the whole idea of an earlier clause or phrase when no misunderstanding is likely.

> The grumbler heard that his boss had called him incompetent. *This* made him resign.

8g Make a pronoun refer clearly to one antecedent, not uncertainly to two.

Uncertain   Melville visited Hawthorne while he was American consul in Liverpool.

Clear While Hawthorne was American consul in Liverpool, Melville visited him.

8h Use pronouns ending in *-self* or *-selves* only in sentences that contain antecedents for the pronouns.

An **intensive pronoun** is a pronoun ending in *-self* or *-selves* and used to emphasize a noun or pronoun.

She **herself** will take the money to the bank.

The intensive pronoun *herself* emphasizes the pronoun *She*. Sometimes, however, intensive pronouns are used incorrectly.

Faulty He invited my sister and *myself* to the play.
Right He invited my sister and *me* to the play.

Because there is no *I* in the sentence for the intensive pronoun *myself* to refer to, it must be replaced by the personal pronoun *me*.

• *Exercise 11*

Decide how to correct each vague or incorrect pronoun reference. Identify the sentence that is correct as written.

1. Each of the female flight attendants decided that they would remain with the damaged aircraft.

2. On or before April 15 most American citizens file their income tax returns.

3. No matter what the detergent commercials say, no woman is really jubilant at the prospect of mopping their dirty kitchen floor.

4. The drifter, along with his many irresponsible relatives, never paid back a cent they borrowed.

5. Neither the batter nor the fans hesitated to show his ardent disapproval of the umpire's decision.

6. Every boy looks forward to the time when they will be a man.

7. The League of Nations failed because they never received full support from the member countries.

8. Did the officer hand the citation to yourself or to your passenger?

9. Neither of the two women ever admitted their guilt, but the police strongly suspected one of them of poisoning several people.

10. John introduced James to me when he was a sophomore.

- ## *Exercise 12*

  Decide how to correct each vague or faulty pronoun reference.

  1. The average factory worker is now well paid, but they have not been able to do much about the boredom.

  2. They tell you that you must pay taxes, but most of the time you do not know what they use your money for.

  3. In the highly competitive world of advertising, those who do not have it are soon passed over for promotion.

4. They use much less silver now in coins, so they are worth less in themselves as well as in what they buy.

5. Mail service has not improved over the years although it has gone up.

6. The lifeguard which saved the two children did not learn to swim until she was eighteen.

7. Some people claim that it is almost meaningless to send greeting cards, but others believe that it is worth preserving.

8. David fought Goliath although he was much smaller in size and was not an experienced warrior.

9. The poet is widely admired, but it is very difficult indeed to make a living at it.

10. At present there are thousands of people trying to escape unemployment, yet they cannot find it in the cities.

9 Case

Use correctly the case forms of pronouns and the possessive case forms of nouns.

English has remnants of three cases: subjective, possessive, and objective. Nouns change their forms only in the possessive *(father, father's)*. Some pronouns, notably the personal pronouns *(I,* etc.) and the relative pronoun *who,* take their form according to their case *(I; my, mine; me).*

To determine case, find how a word is used in its own clause—for example, whether it is a subject or a subjective complement (see **7i**), a possessive, or an object.

9a

9a Use the subjective case for subjects and subjective complements.

> **Subjects** This month *he and I* have not been inside the library. (Never *him and me*)
>
> It looked as if *she and I* were going to be blamed. (Never *her and me*)

Subjective Complements The two guilty ones were *you and I.*

In conversation *you and me* is sometimes used instead of *you and I* for the subjective complement. In speech *it's me* is almost universally accepted. *It's us, it's him,* and *it's her* are also common.

9b

9b Use the objective case for the object of a preposition.

> **Faulty** The manager had to choose *between* he and I.
>
> **Right** The manager had to choose *between* him and me.

Between is a preposition—a connective word, like *into* or *of,* that joins a noun or pronoun to the rest of the sentence—and therefore demands an object.

Be careful about the case of pronouns in constructions like the following:

> **Faulty** A few *of* we boys learned how to cook.
>
> **Right** A few *of* us boys learned how to cook.

When in doubt, test by dropping the noun (not *of we,* but *of us*).

9c   Use the objective case for the subject of an infinitive.

subject
↓
The reporter considered **her** *to be* the best swimmer in the pool.

9d   An appositive and the word it refers to should be in the same case.

An **appositive** is a word, phrase, or clause used as a noun and placed beside another word to explain it. Pronoun appositives take different cases depending on the case of the word they refer to.

Subjective   Two *members* of the committee—Bill and I—were appointed by the chairperson.

Objective   He appointed two *members*—Bill and me.

9e   The case of a pronoun after *than* or *as* in an elliptical (incomplete) clause should be the same as if the clause were completely expressed.

understood
↓
No one else in the play was as versatile as **she** *(was)*.

understood
↓
The director admired no one else as much as *(he did)* **her**.

9f   Use the possessive case for most pronouns preceding a gerund (*-ing* word derived from a verb and used as a noun); a noun before a gerund may be possessive or objective.

My *driving* does not delight my father.
I don't mind **Mary's** *knowing* the secret.

The noun is objective in certain instances:

1. When a phrase intervenes:

   Regulations prevented the **family** of a sailor *meeting* him at the dock.

2. When a noun preceding the gerund is plural:

   There is no rule against **employees** *working* overtime.

3. When a noun is abstract:

   I object to **emotion** *overruling* judgment.

4. When a noun denotes an inanimate object:

   The crew did object to the **ship** *staying* in port.

When the *-ing* word is a participle (used as an adjective) and not a gerund, the noun or pronoun preceding it is in the objective case.

I heard **him** *singing* loudly.
I hear **you** *calling* me.

9g Use an *of*-phrase to indicate the possessive with abstractions or inanimate objects.

Incongruous The building's construction was delayed.
  Preferred The construction of the building was delayed.

There are well-established exceptions: *a stone's throw, for pity's sake, a month's rest, heart's desire, a day's work.*

9h The possessive forms of personal pronouns do not have an apostrophe; the possessive forms of indefinite pronouns have an apostrophe.

Personal Pronouns   *yours, its, hers, his, ours, theirs*
Indefinite Pronouns   *everyone's, other's, one's, anybody else's*

NOTE   Contractions, such as *it's (it is), he's,* and *she's,* require an apostrophe.

9i   The case of an interrogative or a relative pronoun is determined by its use in its own clause.

Interrogative pronouns (used in questions) are *who, whose, whom, what,* and *which.* **Relative pronouns** are *who, whose, whom, what, which, that,* and the forms with *-ever,* such as *whoever* and *whosoever.* Those which give difficulty through change in form are *who* and *whoever* (subjective) and *whom* and *whomever* (objective).

The case of these pronouns is clear in uncomplicated sentences.

Who *defeated* Richard III?

But when something (usually a subordinate clause) intervenes between the pronoun and the rest of the clause, its function is sometimes obscured:

Who do the history books say *defeated* Richard III?

Use two simple ways to tell the case of the pronoun in such sentences:

1. Mentally cancel the intervening words.

   Who ~~do the history books say~~ defeated Richard III?

2. Rearrange the sentence in declarative order: subject — verb — complement.

   The history books do say who defeated Richard III.

A similar procedure will work in determining when *whom* should be used.

NOTE   In speech *who* is usually the form used at the beginning of a sentence.

> **Who** were you talking *to* over there?

The case of a relative pronoun is determined by its use in its own clause, not by the case of its antecedent. Use these three easy steps to check this usage.

1. Pick out the relative clause and draw a box around it.

> This is the child $\boxed{\text{(who, whom) the artist said was his model.}}$

2. Cancel intervening expressions (*he says, it is reported,* and so on).

> This is the child $\boxed{\text{(who, whom) }\cancel{\text{the artist said}}\text{ was his model.}}$

3. Find the verb in the relative clause.

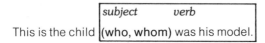

NOTE   Do not confuse the function of the relative pronoun in its clause with the function of the clause as a whole.

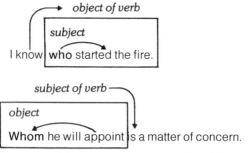

Try to avoid writing sentences with elaborate clauses using *who* and *whom*.

• Exercise 13

Choose the correct form in each of the following sentences.

1. No one knows the penalty for cheating better than *(he, him.)*
2. On the platform stood the man *(who, whom)* they all believed had practiced witchcraft.
3. On the platform stood the man *(who, whom)* they all accused of practicing witchcraft.
4. The first two speakers will be you and *(she, her).*
5. The person *(who, whom)* would be great of soul must first know poverty and suffering.
6. Wise spending is essential to *(us, we)* poor students.
7. On skid row is a little mission which gives *(whoever, whomever)* comes a hot meal, a dry place to sleep, and a word of encouragement.
8. Will the delegate from Hawaii please indicate *(who, whom)* she wants to support?
9. It was *(him, he)* who discovered the fossils in the Olduvai Gorge.
10. Truth is there for *(whoever, whomever)* will seek it.

• Exercise 14

Decide how to correct each incorrect form in the following sentences.

1. The speaker said that him and the wilderness guide were the ones most afraid of the white water on the trip downriver.

2. The Navajo and the tourist walked behind the display booth. After much discussion between he and she, it was

finally agreed that the first chance to buy the turquoise bracelet was her's.

3. No one was able to make more intricate sand designs than him.

4. The mayor chose two councilpersons—she and I—to select the speaker for the next meeting.

5. "You and me," the elderly artisan said, "will construct an intricate firework which will burst into a colorful design."

6. It was a good days work to repair the house's roof.

7. Deep thinkers have motives and secrets that us ordinary people can never fathom.

8. The visitor spoke to my sister and I.

9. Its true that the Potomac got it's name from the Native American.

10. I apologized because I wanted no ill feelings between he and I.

10 Adjectives and Adverbs

Adjectives modify nouns and pronouns. Adverbs modify verbs, adjectives, and other adverbs.

Most adverbs end in -ly, whereas only a few adjectives (lovely, holy, manly, friendly) have this ending. Some adverbs have two forms, one with -ly and one without: slow and slowly, loud and loudly. Most adverbs are formed by adding -ly to adjectives: warm, warmly; pretty, prettily.

10a

Choosing correct adjectives and adverbs in some sentences is no problem.

> The barber gave him a *close* shave.
> Study the text *closely.*

Avoid using adjectives to modify verbs, adverbs, or other adjectives. Distinguish between *sure* and *surely, easy* and *easily, good* and *well, real* and *really.*

Not A real *good* high jumper *soars* over the bar *easy.*

But A really *good* high jumper *soars* over the bar *easily.*

10a Form the comparative and superlative degrees of most short adjectives and some adverbs by adding *-er* and *-est.* Use *more* and *most* (or *less* and *least*) before long adjectives, participles, and most adverbs.

		Comparative	**Superlative**
Adjectives	dear	dearer	dearest
	pretty	prettier	prettiest
	but pitiful	more pitiful	most pitiful
	grasping	more grasping	most grasping
Adverbs	slow	slower	slowest
	but rapidly	more rapidly	most rapidly

Consult your dictionary if you are in doubt about correct comparative and superlative forms.

Strictly speaking, some adjectives and adverbs are absolute; that is, they cannot be compared (*dead, perfect, complete, unique*). A thing cannot, logically, be more or less dead, or perfect, or unique (one of a kind). In formal writing use *more nearly perfect.*

10b Use the comparative to refer to two things; the superlative, to more than two.

> *Both* cars are fast, but the small car is (the) faster.
> All *three* cars are fast, but the small car is (the) fastest.

10c Use a predicate adjective, not an adverb, after a linking verb, such as *be, seem, become, look, appear, feel, sound, smell, taste.*

Words like *good* and *bad* are adjectives and can be used after linking verbs to describe the subject.

> *He* feels **bad.** (He is ill or depressed.)

> He *reads* **badly.** (*Reads* expresses an action; it is not a linking verb.)

> The *tea* tasted **sweet.** (*Sweet* describes the tea.)

> She *tasted* the tea **daintily.** (*Daintily* tells how she tasted the tea.)

10d

Use an adjective, not an adverb, to follow a verb and its object when the modifier refers to the object, not to the verb.

Verbs like *keep, build, hold, dig, make, think* can have an object and an object complement. After verbs of this kind choose the adjective or the adverb form carefully.

> Keep your *clothes* **neat.** (Adjective—modifies complement)

Keep your clothes **neatly** in the closet. (Adverb—modifies verb)

Make my *bed* **soft**.

Make the bed **carefully**.

• Exercise 15

Decide which form of the adverb or adjective is correct in each of the following sentences.

1. The nautilus is the most *(unique, nearly unique)* species of sea animal.
2. The ancient Thracians transported their gold and silver treasures *(easy, easily)*.
3. The construction workers made the room *(snug, snugly)*.
4. Of the two civilizations, Toltec and Aztec, the Aztec was the *(later, latest)*.
5. Several students are *(real, really)* interested in DNA research.
6. He feels *(bad, badly)* that he did not get the job.
7. In the old camelback trunk the souvenirs of the last century had been kept *(safe, safely)* from harm.
8. His serve is *(more perfect, more nearly perfect)* than hers.
9. The bagpipe is a *(complexer, more complex)* musical instrument than the dulcimer.
10. Of the three runners, she was *(faster, fastest)*.

• Exercise 16

Identify unacceptable forms of adjectives and adverbs, and supply the correct form in each case. Note: some sentences are correct as written.

10d

1. Socrates thought deep about the nature and purpose of humanity.

2. Even though you may feel bad about past acts, they can never be changed.

3. The young coach was real angry about the commissioner's decision to fine him.

4. The ambassador spoke so rapid that no one interpreted her accurate.

5. It sure cannot be denied that Tennyson was one of the popularest poets of his time.

6. The computer, a real complicated mechanical mind, is the most unique instrument of modern civilization.

7. The manager, a woman of decision, always seemed to know which of two possibilities was best.

8. The plastic bag kept the sandwiches fresh.

9. The golfer's score was only average, but since she had often done poorly, she felt good about it.

10. Of the two high schools, which has the most students going on to college?

Sentence Structure

11 Excessive Coordination

Do not string together a number of short independent clauses.

Wordiness and monotony result from brief independent clauses connected by coordinating conjunctions (*and, and so, but, or, nor, for, yet, so*). Excessive coordination fails to show precise relationships between thoughts. Skillful writers use subordinating connectives like *although, because, since, so that, until, unless,* and *before* and such relative pronouns as *who* and *which.*

Stringy   The mountain is six thousand feet high, *and* it is only four miles from the airport, *and* the field is not a very large one, *but* no plane has ever crashed on it.

Make the last clause the central idea, and condense the sentence by using subordinating elements.

Improved   Although the airport is small and a six-thousand-foot mountain is only four miles away, no plane has ever crashed on the field.

- *Exercise 1*

Decide how the excessive coordination in the following sentences could be eliminated by subordinating some of the ideas.

1. Pagodas are found in several Eastern countries, and they often have many stories and upward-curving roofs.

2. Sharks are ferocious, and they attack many bathers each year, but they seldom kill; their reputation as killers is in part undeserved.

3. Some vacationers leave home in search of quiet, so they find a place without a telephone or television; but other people want complete isolation, and they discover that it is difficult to find a state park that is not crowded with campers and tents.

4. The English teacher gave the new student an assignment and he had to write just one sentence, but he could not think of an interesting subject, and so he did not do the required work.

5. Famous books are not always written by admirable people, for some authors are arrogant, and some are even immoral.

6. The manta ray has a wide, flat body, and it is a member of the same class of fish as the shark.

7. Headhunters still exist in remote areas of the world, but

they are rapidly disappearing, and we seldom hear of them today.

8. Computers calculate rapidly, and they do more work than a human being in the same time, and they threaten many jobs, but we must use these machines.

9. Women have been discriminated against, and in the past they have been patient, but now they are protesting, and their cause is just.

10. Benjamin Franklin was an American, but he was at home wherever he went, and so he gained wide popularity in France, and he was also well known in England.

12 Subordination

Use subordinate clauses (dependent clauses) accurately and effectively to avoid excessive coordination and also to achieve variety and emphasis.

Insufficient or excessive subordination may ruin style or create excessively long and stringy sentences (see also **11**). Selection of the proper thought to subordinate reveals the relative importance of ideas in a sentence.

12a Express main ideas in independent clauses, less important ideas in subordinate clauses.

An optimistic sociologist, who might wish to stress progress despite crime, would write:

Although the crime rate is very high, society has progressed in many ways.

A pessimistic sociologist might wish the opposite emphasis:

> Although society has progressed in many ways, the crime rate is very high.

12b Avoid excessive overlapping of subordinate constructions.

Monotony and even confusion can result from a series of clauses with each depending on the previous one.

Overlapping   A watch is an intricate mechanism

which measures time,

which many people regard as the gift

that is most precious.

Improved   A watch is an intricate mechanism made to measure time, which many people regard as the most precious gift.

• Exercise 2

The following is an exercise in thinking and relationships, designed to point up differences in meaning that result from subordination. Read the pairs of sentences carefully and answer the questions.

1. A. After the Roman Empire was considerably weakened, corruption in high places became widespread.
   B. After corruption in high places became widespread, the Roman Empire was considerably weakened.

   Which of these sentences would a historian writing on the causes of Rome's fall be more likely to write?

2. A. Although a lifetime is short, much can be accomplished.
   B. Although much can be accomplished, a lifetime is short.

   Which of these sentences expresses more determination?

3. A. When in doubt, most drivers apply the brakes.
   B. When most drivers apply the brakes, they are in doubt.

   With which drivers would you prefer to ride?

4. A. In spite of the fact that he had a speech defect, Cotton Mather became a great preacher.
   B. In spite of the fact that he became a great preacher, Cotton Mather had a speech defect.

   In which sentence did he apparently overcome the defect?
   In which sentence did the defect remain noticeable?

5. A. While taking a bath, Archimedes formulated one of the most important principles in physics.
   B. While formulating one of the most important principles in physics, Archimedes took a bath.

   Which sentence indicates accidental discovery?

• *Exercise 3*

Decide how the following sentences might be rewritten to avoid overlapping subordination.

1. *Hamlet* is a play by Shakespeare that tells of a prince who has difficulty making up his mind to avenge the murder of his father.

2. Each musician who plays in the orchestra which performs in the club that is on the side of the lake has at least fifteen years of professional experience.

3. Lobster Newburg is a dish which consists of cooked lobster meat which is heated in a chafing dish which contains a special cream sauce.

4. Few people who smoke realize that the tobacco used in ordinary cigarettes is of the same family as nightshade, which is poisonous.

5. Between the sixth and seventh floors the elevator stuck that had the board member who could have cast a vote that would have changed the future of the corporation.

13 Completeness
Make your sentences complete in structure and thought.

Sentences should be clear, and every element should be expressed or implied clearly enough to prevent misunderstanding. Do not omit necessary verbs, conjunctions, and prepositions.

13a Make constructions with *so, such,* and *too* complete.

To avoid misunderstanding, be sure that the idea is expressed completely.

Not Clear The boy was too short. (Too short for what?)
   Clear The boy was too short to play center.

Not Clear	Those coins were so rare. (So rare that what?)
Clear	Those coins were so rare that even an expert could not identify them.

13b Do not omit a verb or a preposition which is necessary to the meaning of the sentence.

Logic or idiom—what sounds natural—sometimes demands two different forms.

Not She was simultaneously *repelled* and *drawn* toward the city. *(Repelled* toward?*)*

But She was simultaneously *repelled* by and *drawn* toward the city.

Better She was simultaneously *repelled* by the city and *drawn* toward it.

Not In the confusion the *silver coins* were scattered and the *paper money* stolen. (Paper money *were* stolen?)

But In the confusion the *silver coins* were scattered, and the *paper money* was stolen.

However, when the same form is called for in both elements, it need not be repeated:

To err is human; to forgive, divine.

13c Omission of *that* sometimes obscures meaning.

Not Clear	The systems analyst found a happy worker is an efficient worker.
Clear	The systems analyst found *that* a happy worker is an efficient worker.

14

- *Exercise 4*

  Decide how to correct any errors in completeness. Note: not all of the sentences contain errors.

  1. This sentence is a little different.
  2. Happy workers always have and still do produce the best results.
  3. The lighthouse stood as a symbol and guide to safety.
  4. Some parents are so lax that they allow their children almost unlimited freedom.
  5. The editor says that the headlines have been written and the type set.
  6. The flooding river was so wide, so powerful, and so uncontrollable.
  7. The children enjoyed singing a song about going over the river and the woods.
  8. The gardener knew a plant which grows in the air without roots requires little attention.
  9. In the morning he felt so sick.
  10. Sherlock Holmes always has and still does represent the the ideal British detective.

14 Comparisons

Make comparisons logical and clear.

Compare only similar terms.

The *laughter* of a loon is more frightening than an **owl**.

This sentence compares a sound and a bird. A consistent sentence would compare sound and sound or bird and bird.

The *laughter* of a loon is more frightening than the **hoot** of an owl.

A *loon* is more frightening than an **owl**.

The word *other* is often needed in a comparison:

Illogical The Sahara is larger than any desert in the world.
Right The Sahara is larger than any *other* desert in the world.

Avoid awkward and incomplete comparisons.

Awkward and The lily is *as white*, if not whiter **than,** any other
Incomplete flower. *(As white* requires *as,* not *than.)*

Better The lily is *as* white *as* any other flower, if not whiter. (*Than any other* is understood.)

Awkward and Yellowstone National Park is one of the most beau-
Incomplete tiful, if not the most beautiful, national park. (After
one of the most beautiful, the plural *parks* is required.)
Better Yellowstone National Park is one of the most beautiful national parks, if not the most beautiful.
Or Yellowstone is one of the most beautiful national
parks.

Not Clear After many years my teacher remembered me better than my friend. (Better than she remembered
my friend, or better than my friend remembered me?)
Clear After many years my teacher remembered me better than she did my friend.

Feeble *Catch-22* is different.

Clear *Catch-22* is different from other war novels of its time.

• *Exercise 5*

Decide how to correct any errors in comparisons.

1. When Alexander the Great was young, he swore to hate Rome more than any person.

2. Visitors to New Lawson discover that the summers there are as hot, if not hotter than, any they have ever experienced.

3. Some people go to Florida every winter because they feel that the winter climate is better than any state.

4. The baboons ate more of the bananas than the ants.

5. The veterinarian read a learned article proving that horses like dogs better than cats.

6. For one's health plain water is as good, if not better than, most liquids.

7. The telephone is one of the most useful, if not the most useful, instruments in modern life.

8. The storms of the Black Sea are more severe than the Aegean.

9. Museums in Boston and Washington have larger collections of Oriental art than any in the United States.

10. The tulips of Pakistan are not as famous as Holland.

15 Consistency

Write sentences which maintain grammatical consistency.

Unnecessary changes in grammatical forms are misleading and annoying.

15a Avoid unnecessary shifts between past and present tense.

Shifts in tense most frequently occur in narration.

Needless Shift from Present to Past
The architect *plans* the new stadium, and then the mayor *decided* not to build it.

Needless Shift from Past to Present
The social worker in the novel *made* extensive plans to accomplish reforms, but all her efforts *come* to nothing.

Also avoid needless shifts between conditional forms *(should, would, could)* and other verb forms.

Not Exhaustion after a vacation *could* be avoided if a family *can* plan better. (Use either sequence, *could . . . would* or *can . . . can.*)

15b Avoid careless shifts in personal pronouns.

Faulty In felling a tree, a lumberjack first cuts a deep notch near the bottom of the trunk and on the side toward which *he* wishes the tree to fall. Then *you* saw on the other side, directly opposite the notch.

Correct In felling a tree, *you* first cut a deep notch near the bottom of the trunk and on the side toward which *you* wish the tree to fall. Then *you* saw on the other side, directly opposite the notch.

Or In felling a tree, a lumberjack first cuts a deep notch near the bottom of the trunk and on the side toward which *he* wishes the tree to fall. Then *he* saws on the other side, directly opposite the notch.

15c Avoid unnecessary shifts in mood (see **6**).

subjunctive
↓
Shifts It is necessary that the applicant *fill* in this form

indicative
↓
and *mails* it.

Consistent It is necessary that the applicant *fill* in this form and
Subjunctive *mail* it.

imperative
↓
Shifts First *mail* the application; then the applicant

indicative
↓
will go for an interview.

Consistent First *mail* the application; then *go* for an interview.
Imperative

15d Avoid unnecessary shifts in voice (see **5**).

Poor The chef *cooks* **(active)** the shrimp casserole for thirty minutes and then it *is allowed* **(passive)** to cool.

Better The chef *cooks* the shrimp casserole for thirty minutes then *allows* it to cool.

15e Avoid unnecessary shifts from one relative pronoun to another.

Shift She went to the cupboard *that* leaned perilously forward and *which* always resisted every attempt to open it.

Consistent She went to the cupboard *which* leaned perilously forward and *which* always resisted every attempt to open it. (Or, *that . . . that*)

15f Avoid a shift from indirect to direct discourse in the same construction.

Indirect discourse paraphrases (expresses in another way) the speaker's words; direct discourse quotes exactly.

Mixed ←——————— *indirect* ———————→
He says that the book is trashy and

←———————*direct* ———————→
why would anyone wish to read it?

Indirect He says that the book is trashy and asks why anyone would wish to read it.

Direct He says, "The book is trashy. Why would anyone wish to read it?"

● *Exercise 6*

Decide how the shifts in grammar in the following sentences might best be corrected.

1. The representative rose slowly, cleared her throat, and moved that the motion be tabled and that the meeting is adjourned.

2. A boy who writes an appealing letter to his girlfriend will seem to have an attractive personality, but the next time you see her you must be as interesting in person as you are when you write.

3. The failures in the experiments will be avoided this time if the assistants would follow the instructions precisely.

4. The retreating actor backed out of the door, jumped on a horse, and rides off into the sunset.

5. The social studies teacher was dismayed because at the end of last year seven students still cannot discuss the Civil War intelligently.

6. The girl that won the contest is the one who lives next door.

7. You do the filming with the motion picture camera, and then the film is quickly developed inside the camera.

8. The curator told me of her interest in Native American art and would you like to see the collection?

9. The play is still running, as any visitor to New York could witness.

10. Half of the researchers follow the guidelines scrupulously; the others cared little about correct procedures.

16 Position of Modifiers
Place modifiers so that they clearly attach to the right word or element in the sentence.

16a

A poorly placed modifier which attaches to the wrong word can create confusion, misunderstanding, or absurdity.

16a Avoid dangling modifiers.

Many danglers are verbal phrases (see Glossary) at the beginning of a sentence.

Dangling Participle

Running along the street, my *face* felt frozen. (Who was running? My face? Of course not; I was running.)

Clear

Running along the street, *I* felt as if my face were frozen.

Or

As I ran along the street, my face *felt* frozen. (The participial phrase has been changed to an adverbial clause which modifies *felt*.)

Dangling Gerund

After **searching** around the attic, a *diary* was discovered. (Who did the searching? The diary? Of course not; a person did the searching.)

Clear

After **searching** around the attic, *I* discovered a diary.

Dangling Infinitive

To **enter** the house, the *lock* on the back door was picked. (*To enter the house* refers to no word in this sentence.)

Clear

To **enter** the house, *he* picked the lock on the back door.

Dangling Prepositional Phrase

With **great eagerness** the laboratory *experiment* began. (Who was eager? The experiment? Of course not; the researcher.)

Clear

With great eagerness the *researcher* began the laboratory experiment.

Clause with Omitted Words

While still sleepy and tired, the *counselor* lectured me on breaking rules.

Clear

While I was still sleepy and tired, the counselor lectured me on
breaking rules.

NOTE   Some verbal phrases need not refer to a single word in
the sentence.

> *Strictly speaking,* does this sentence contain a dangling con-
> struction?

> *To tell the truth,* it does not.

The phrases are sentence modifiers.

16b   Avoid misplaced modifiers.

The placement of a modifier in a sentence affects meaning.

> He enlisted after he married *again.*
> He enlisted *again* after he married.

Almost any modifier which comes between an adjective clause
and the word it modifies can cause awkwardness or misunderstanding.

Faulty   Wordsworth addressed a passage to his friend Coleridge
in *The Prelude,* who collaborated with him in writing
Lyrical Ballads.

Clear In *The Prelude* Wordsworth addressed a passage to his friend Coleridge, who collaborated with him in writing *Lyrical Ballads*.

Faulty Some insecticides are still used on crops that are suspected of being dangerous.

Clear Some insecticides that are suspected of being dangerous are still used on crops.

16c A modifier placed between two words so that it seems to modify either word is said to "squint."

Unclear The horse which was pawing *viciously* kicked its owner.

Clear The horse which was *viciously pawing* kicked its owner.

Or The horse which was pawing *kicked* its owner *viciously*.

• *Exercise 7*

Decide how to correct the faulty modifiers in the following sentences.

1. Looking through a telescope the moon could be seen clearly.

2. The courageous patient was able to walk about two weeks after the accident.

3. This computer is seldom used even though it is very effective because of the high cost.

4. To be absolutely certain the answer must be checked.

5. The restaurant offers special meals for children that are in-expensive.

6. Serve one of the melons for dessert at lunch; keep one of them for the picnic in the refrigerator.

7. My sister inspected the board before sawing for nails.

8. At the age of five my grandfather told me about his life as a soldier.

9. Having been found guilty of drunken driving, the judge sentenced the operator of the car to ninety days in jail.

10. The woman who was writing hastily rose from the desk and left the room.

• *Exercise 8*

Decide how to correct the faulty modifiers in the following sentences.

1. Taking the cat food from the refrigerator, Cleopatra began to purr loudly.

2. Without shoes the rough stones cut the feet of the hikers.

3. Although rebellious, the bridge was nevertheless built by the construction workers.

4. To taste really good, the chef should prepare a suitable dressing for the raw spinach salad.

5. The editor only told me that lighthearted columns would be accepted for the children's page.

6. The boat that was rocking violently threw the skipper to the deck.

7. Using a vast array of electronic devices, accurate information is transmitted everywhere.

8. Digging clay for bricks, the Bulgarian treasure was discovered by some workers.

9. Yesterday I only saw a dozen people entering the theater.

10. Approaching the deer, one of them pranced toward us.

17 Separation of Elements

Do not unnecessarily or excessively separate closely related elements.

Separation of subject and verb, parts of a verb phrase, verb and object, and other related sentence elements can be awkward or misleading.

Awkward Wild dogs had, *for several sleet-ridden and storm-ravaged winter days when the marrow seemed to freeze in the bones and food was scarce,* been seen on the hills.

Improved *For several sleet-ridden and storm-ravaged winter days when the marrow seemed to freeze in the bones and food was scarce,* wild dogs had been seen on the hills.

Absurd She is the man who owns the service station's wife.

Accurate She is the wife of the man who owns the service station.

Split infinitives occur when a modifier comes between *to* and the verb form, as in *to loudly complain.* Some grammarians ban them without exception. Others insist that some split infinitives are more graceful than possible alternatives. To avoid objections, you would be wise not to split infinitives.

Unnecessary He felt it *to really be* impossible.
Preferable He felt it *to be* really impossible.

• *Exercise 9*

Decide how the following sentences might be revised to avoid the separation of closely related elements.

1. It is unwise to hastily judge other people.

2. They could reconstruct from family memories passed on by her granddaughter the life of a courageous farm woman during the Civil War.

3. We found in junkshops and antique stores the old-fashioned lamps.

4. Money to totally fund the project came from a national foundation.

5. Fanny Cobb Carter had as a young girl seen at the home of her grandmother Booker T. Washington.

6. He was made a trustee of an organization that over the years has rescued numerous historical sites and scenic landscapes, the Heritage Preservation Association.

7. He is the woman who owns the variety store's husband.

8. If you want to properly make a gravestone rubbing, you can follow these guidelines.

9. Overfishing or overgrazing can for generations to come destabilize an environment.

10. Asian Americans came at different times and under different circumstances to the United States.

18 Parallelism

Use parallel grammatical forms to express elements that are parallel in thought. Constructions should be parallel in form if they are connected by coordinating conjunctions *(and, but, or, nor)* or by correlative conjunctions *(either . . . or, neither . . . nor, not . . . but, not only . . . but also, both . . . and).*

Words go with similar words, phrases with similar phrases, clauses with similar clauses.

Not Parallel
The sheriff was famous for *much talking* and *no action.*

Parallel
The sheriff was famous for *much talk* and *no action.*

Not Parallel
The collector promises
{ *to buy a copy* of the rare book
and
that the cost will not be excessive.

Parallel
The collector promises
{ *that she* will buy a copy of the rare book
and
that the cost will not be excessive.

Awkward Correlatives   *verb*   *pronoun*
The reactionary *not only* supported tyranny *but also* he became a tyrant.

Parallel

verb   *verb*

The reactionary *not only* supported tyranny *but also* became a tyrant.

Do not make elements parallel in a structure when they are
not parallel in thought.

Misleading   At the end of the season the management quietly
Parallelism   closed the hotel, boarded up its windows, and
                  burned a month later.

• Exercise 10

*Decide how the following sentences might be revised as
necessary to eliminate faulty parallelism. Note: not all of
the sentences are incorrect.*

1. The ideal piecrust is tender, flaky, and, of course, tastes
   good.

2. Advertisements promise that small foreign cars are economical and how easy they are to park.

3. Adjusting to a large high school can be difficult for a person who has always attended a small school and being
   used to more individual attention.

4. Roaming through the great north woods, camping by a
   lake, and getting away from crowds are good ways to forget the cares of civilization.

5. To be a good listener, one must have a genuine interest in
   people, a strong curiosity, and discipline oneself to keep
   the mind from wandering.

6. *Death of a Salesman* is a play about a man who has wasted his life and which teaches the need for self-discovery.

7. A good trial lawyer must be well educated in the profession and something of an actor.

8. The delegation found it impossible either to see the governor or even her secretary.

9. Most slow readers could read much faster and better if they would not glance back over lines they have passed and also moving their lips when they read.

10. The jaguar is swift, quiet, and moves with grace.

19 Variety

Vary sentences in length, structure, and order.

Length   An unbroken series of short sentences may become monotonous and fail to indicate such relationships as cause, condition, concession, time sequence, and purpose.

Choppy   Overpopulation is becoming a problem. Alaska is not thickly populated. Many people may move there. It has vast open lands.

These sentences can be combined into one sentence which shows more exactly the relationships of the thoughts.

Improved   Alaska, a relatively unpopulous state, has vast open lands which may attract many people in this time of overpopulation.

Structure   Do not overuse one kind of sentence structure. Write simple sentences (one independent clause and no dependent clauses), compound sentences (at least two independent clauses joined by a word like *and*), and complex sentences (one independent clause and at least one dependent clause). (For more information see the Glossary entries for Complex, compound sentences and Dependent clause.) Vary your sentences among loose, periodic, and balanced forms.

A **loose sentence,** the most frequently used kind, makes its main point early and then adds refinements. In contrast, a **periodic sentence** withholds an element of the main thought until the end to create suspense and emphasis.

> **Loose**   We have made mistakes with our children, which will undoubtedly become clearer as they get old enough to write their own books.   JEAN KERR

> **Loose**   We cannot watch too attentively for the first symptoms of tyranny; when it has grown to a certain point, there is no more time to stop it.
>
> MADAME DE STAËL

> **Periodic**   Under a government which imprisons any unjustly, the true place for a just man is also a prison.
>
> HENRY DAVID THOREAU

> **Periodic**   There is one thing above all others that the scientist has a duty to teach to the public and to governments: it is the duty of heresy.   J. BRONOWSKI

A **balanced sentence** has parts which are similar in structure and length and which express parallel thoughts. Indeed, balance is simply another word for refined and extended parallelism. (For a discussion of parallel structure see **18**.) The following sentence from Ecclesiastes is nearly symmetrical: "That which is crooked cannot be made straight: and that which is wanting cannot be numbered."

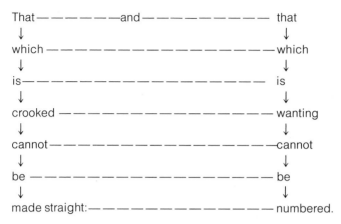

A sentence can also be balanced if only parts of it are symmetrical: "Thus the Puritan was made up of two different men, the one all self-abasement, penitence, gratitude, passion; the other proud, calm, inflexible, sagacious" (THOMAS BABINGTON MACAULAY).

Thus
the Puritan
was made up
of two different men,

the one ——————the other
all self-abasement, —————— proud,
penitence,——————— calm,
gratitude, —————— inflexible,
passion; —————— sagacious.

Order If all sentences follow the normal order of subject-verb-complement, the effect can be monotonous. For interest and emphasis invert the order occasionally, and do not always tack all dependent clauses and long phrases on at the end. Study the variations in the following sentences.

Normal Order

subject   verb   object   modifiers
   ↓   ↓   ↓

She attributed these *defects* in her son's character to the general weaknesses of humanity.

Sentence Beginning with Direct Object

These *defects* in her son's character she attributed to the general weaknesses of humanity.

Sentence Beginning with Prepositional Phrase

To the general weaknesses of humanity she attributed the defects in her son's character.

Sentence Beginning with Adverb

Quickly the swordfish broke the surface of the water.

Inverted Sentence Beginning with Clause Used as Object

That the engineer tried to avert the catastrophe, none of them would deny.

Inverted Sentence Beginning with Dependent Adverbial Clause

If you wish to create a college, therefore, and are wise, you will seek to create a life.   WOODROW WILSON

Sentence Beginning with Participial Phrase

Flying low over the water for hours, the plane searched for survivors.

In climactic order the elements of a series are arranged according to increasing importance. Ordering by decreasing importance may result in anticlimax and loss of emphasis.

Unemphatic	The hurricane left thousands of people homeless, ruined the crops, and interrupted transportation.
Climactic	The hurricane interrupted transportation, ruined the crops, and left thousands of people homeless.

• *Exercise 11*

Decide how one sentence could be made out of each of the groups below.

1. At the age of seventeen I went to debate at a high school.
   Three girls went with me.
   It was the fall of my senior year.
   The high school was over a hundred miles away.

   ADAPTED FROM JOHN UPDIKE

2. There is, indeed, much wrong with cities.
   Big ones and littles ones have problems.
   They should not be abandoned.
   We should not rebuild them on abstract principles.

   ADAPTED FROM ROBERT MOSES

3. Philadelphia is one of America's most historic cities.
   At present it is involved in a program of urban renewal.
   This program is already showing substantial results.

4. Van Gogh was a Dutch painter.
   He belonged to the postimpressionist school.
   Van Gogh once cut off his ear with a razor.
   At that time he was in one of his frequent fits of depression.

5. Some people think mountain climbing is silly.
   They do not really understand.
   A mountain climber is meeting a challenge.
   It is a symbolic challenge.
   The mountain represents the seemingly insurmountable obstacles of life.

- *Exercise 12*

  Decide how to make each of the following sentences periodic.

  1. One machine, the typewriter, revolutionized business practices and had a profound influence on the style of many authors.
  2. A sense of humor is one quality no great leader can be without.
  3. Selfishness, some philosophers maintain, is the reason behind every action of any person.
  4. The blue whale is the largest known creature on earth.
  5. He studied when all other possible methods of passing the course proved unworkable.

- *Exercise 13*

  Decide how the following sentences could be rewritten to give them a balanced construction. Identify the sentence that already has a balanced construction.

19

1. The rewards of youth are obvious, but much more subtle are the rewards of age.

2. A successful advertisement surprises and pleases, but not all advertisements are successful because some are merely boring and irritating.

3. Realists know their limitations; romantics know only what they want.

4. A politician is concerned with successful elections, whereas the future of the people is foremost in the mind of a statesman.

5. A trained ear hears many separate instruments in an orchestra, but the melody is usually all that is heard by the untutored ear.

- ## *Exercise 14*

  Decide how the following sentences could be rewritten according to the principles of climactic order.

  1. Our space ship brought back from the strange planet a large animal, two small green people, and a soil sample.

  2. John Quincy Adams served in more than seven political offices; he was, among other things, President of the United States, a Senator, and a Congressman.

  3. Plagues in the Middle Ages were probably the greatest kind

of national disaster; millions of people suffered death, great pain, and economic losses.

4. Cities are faced with countless problems such as crime in the streets, littering, pollution, and traffic jams.

5. Although the controversial speaker tried to proceed, stones thrown at the platform, annoying catcalls, and a barrage of rotten fruit brought an end to the meeting.

• Exercise 15

Decide how the following passage could be rewritten so that the structure of its sentences is more varied.

An Italian, Cristoforo Colombo, discovered America. Another, Amerigo Vespucci, gave it his name. Neither Italians as a people nor Italy as a country had a significant place in the early history of the United States. In 1621 a small group of Italian glassmakers lived in Jamestown. During the colonial period a few men from the Italian peninsula settled in America. They lived in the cities along the Atlantic seaboard. This sprinkling of Italians left no noteworthy mark on the life of the English colonies.

The largest group of Italians to settle in North America consisted of about two hundred people. They were Protestants. They had lived in the valleys of Piedmont. They were usually called Waldensians after Peter Waldo of Lyon. He was a merchant. He founded their sect. They suffered persecution and massacre at home. Then they fled to Holland. From there they sought refuge in the New World. They arrived in New Amsterdam in the spring of 1657. A few weeks after their arrival they moved on to Delaware. There Dutch Protestants purchased land for them. The Italians organized the first government of New Amstel. Later it was called New Castle. Historians know little about these settlers and their movements. They do know they were Italians. They spoke and kept their records in French. They know too that a small band of them also established a settlement at Stony Brook, New York.

ADAPTED FROM ALEXANDER DECONDE, *Half Bitter, Half Sweet: An Excursion into Italian-American History*

Punctuation

20 The Comma

Use commas to reflect structure and to clarify the sense of the sentence.

The comma is chiefly used (1) *to separate* equal elements, such as independent clauses and items in a series, and (2) *to set off,* or enclose, modifiers or parenthetical (explanatory) words, phrases, and clauses. One comma is needed to separate elements in a sentence, but two commas are needed to set off an element. In such a situation the comma is used both *before* and *after.*

Not   This novel, a best seller has no real literary merit.
But   This novel, a best seller, has no real literary merit.

20a   Use a comma to separate independent clauses joined by a coordinating conjunction.

Nice is a word with many meanings, and some of them are opposite to others.

Sherlock Holmes had to be prepared, for Watson was full of questions.

NOTE The comma is sometimes omitted when the clauses are short and there is no danger of misreading.

The weather was clear and the pilot landed.

20b Use a comma between words, phrases, or clauses in a series.

The closet contained worn clothes, old shoes, and dusty hats.

The final comma before *and* in a series is sometimes omitted.

The closet contained worn clothes, old shoes and dusty hats.

But the comma must be used when the final elements could be misread.

An old chest in the corner was filled with nails, hammers, a hacksaw and blades, and a brace and bit.

Series of phrases, of dependent clauses, or of independent clauses are also separated by commas.

Phrases We hunted for the letter in the album, in all the old trunks, and even under the rug.

Dependent Clauses Finally we guessed that the letter had been burned, that someone else had already discovered it, or that it had never been written.

Independent Clauses We left the attic, Father locked the door, and Mother suggested that we never unlock it again.

• *Exercise 1*

Decide where commas need to be inserted in the following sentences.

1. Some women authors took masculine pen names in the nineteenth century for they felt that the public would not read serious works written by women.
2. Good speakers should prepare themselves well speak clearly enough to be understood and practice the art of effective timing.
3. The markings on the wall of the cave were not as ancient as others but none of the experts could interpret them.
4. The hamper was filled with cold cuts bread and butter and mixed pickles.
5. Some government documents are classified secret for the safety of the country must be preserved.
6. The sensitive child knew that the earth was round but she thought that she was on the inside of it.
7. The teacher said that the class had not been doing very well that nearly everyone had failed to take notes and that she wanted to see some improvement.
8. For breakfast he served us bacon and eggs toast and jelly and hot coffee.
9. Careless driving includes speeding stopping suddenly making turns from the wrong lane of traffic going through red lights and so forth.
10. Driving was easy for a great part of the way was paved and traffic was light.

20c Use a comma between coordinate adjectives not joined by *and.* Do not use a comma between cumulative adjectives.

Coordinate adjectives modify the noun independently.

Cumulative ones modify not only the noun but the whole cluster of intervening adjectives. Note the difference:

Coordinate   Madame de Staël was an attractive, gracious lady.

Ferocious, vigilant, loyal dogs were essential to safety in the Middle Ages.

Cumulative   She has short blond hair.

The uninvited guest wore an old navy blue suit.

Two tests are helpful.

Test One   *And* is natural only between coordinate adjectives.

>   an attractive *and* gracious lady
>   ferocious *and* vigilant *and* loyal dogs

Not   short *and* blond hair
old *and* navy *and* blue suit

Test Two   Coordinate adjectives are easily reversible.

>   a gracious, attractive lady
>   loyal, vigilant, ferocious dogs

Not   blond short hair
blue navy old suit

The distinction is not always clear-cut, however, and the sense of the cluster must be the deciding factor.

She was wearing a full-skirted, low-cut velvet gown.

(A velvet gown that was full-skirted and low-cut; not a gown that was full-skirted and low-cut and velvet.)

NOTE   A comma is not used before the noun:

Not   gracious, lady
ferocious, dogs

But   gracious lady
ferocious dogs

- ## *Exercise 2*

  Decide how to punctuate the following. When in doubt apply the tests just described. Note: not all of the expressions require added commas.

  1. a graceful agile cat
  2. large glass doors
  3. a little black address book
  4. a high-crowned lemon-yellow felt hat
  5. a wrinkled brown paper bag
  6. a hot sultry depressing day
  7. the gloomy forbidding night scene
  8. straight strawberry-blond hair
  9. a woebegone ghostly look
  10. beautiful imported Persian rugs

20d   Use a comma after a long introductory phrase or clause.

Long Phrase   With this bitter part of the ordeal behind him, the trapper felt more confident.

Long Clause   When this bitter part of the ordeal was behind him, the trapper felt more confident.

When the introductory element is short and there is no danger of misreading, the comma is often omitted.

20e

Short Phrase   After this ordeal the trapper felt more confident.

Short Clause   When this ordeal was over the trapper felt more confident.

Commas after these introductory elements would be acceptable. Use of the comma in such situations may depend on personal taste.

Introductory verbal phrases (participial, infinitive, and gerund), however, are usually set off by commas.

Participle   Living for centuries, redwoods often reach a height of three hundred feet.

Infinitive   To verify or correct his hypothesis, a scientist performs an experiment.

Gerund   After surviving this ordeal, the trapper felt relieved.

A phrase or a clause set off by a comma at the beginning of a sentence may not require a comma if it is moved to the end of the sentence.

Beginning   Because of pity for creatures that must live in small cages, some people refuse to go to the zoo.

End   Some people refuse to go to the zoo because of pity for creatures that must live in small cages.

20e   Use commas to set off nonrestrictive appositives (explanatory words), phrases, and clauses.

A **nonrestrictive modifier** describes and adds information but does not point out or identify; omit the modifier, and the sentence loses some meaning but does not change radically or become meaningless.

Nonrestrictive   Shakespeare's last play, *The Tempest*, is optimistic and even sunny in mood.

Taxicabs, *which are always expensive*, cost less in Washington than elsewhere.

> Oil, *which is lighter than water*, rises to the surface.

In these sentences the italicized modifiers add information, but they are not essential to the meaning of the sentence.

NOTE   *That* never introduces a nonrestrictive clause.

A **restrictive modifier** points out or identifies its noun or pronoun.

Restrictive   The play *Macbeth* has been a scholar's delight for over three hundred years.

Taxicabs *that are dirty* are illegal in some cities.

Water *which is murky in appearance* should always be boiled before drinking.

In these sentences the italicized expressions identify the words they modify; to remove these modifiers is to change the meaning radically or to make the sentence false.

Some modifiers can be either restrictive or nonrestrictive, and use or omission of the commas changes the sense.

> The coin which gleamed in the sunlight was a Spanish doubloon. (There were several coins.)

> The coin, which gleamed in the sunlight, was a Spanish doubloon. (There was only one coin.)

In speech a nonrestrictive modifier is usually preceded by a pause, whereas a restrictive modifier is not.

• *Exercise 3*

The following pairs of sentences illustrate differences in meaning which result from the use of commas to set off modifiers. Answer the questions about each pair of sentences.

1. A. Her marriage to the architect Warren White ended in divorce.
   B. Her marriage, to the architect Warren White, ended in divorce.

   In which sentence had the woman been married only once?

2. A. The hitchhiker leaning against the post seemed totally indifferent about getting a ride.
   B. The hitchhiker, leaning against the post, seemed totally indifferent about getting a ride.

   How many hitchhikers are there in sentence A? Sentence B?

3. A. The compulsory school law, which has just been passed, insures educational training for all children.
   B. The compulsory school law which has just been passed insures educational training for all children.

   Which sentence refers to a place which has never before had a compulsory school law?

4. A. Young drivers, who are not well trained, cause most of our minor automobile accidents.
   B. Young drivers who are not well trained cause most of our minor automobile accidents.

   Which sentence shows a prejudice against young drivers?

5. A. Anthropologists, who respect tribal cultures, are welcome among most groups.
   B. Anthropologists who respect tribal cultures are welcome among most groups.

   Which sentence reflects confidence in anthropologists?

20f

• *Exercise 4*

Decide where commas need to be added for nonrestrictive modifiers, and identify the unnecessary commas. Note: some sentences are correct as written.

1. The name Rover was often associated with dogs which were stupid and happy.
2. Barbers, who are bald, are frequently the ones who are most authoritative in discussing baldness with their customers, who are worrying about losing their hair.
3. The wealthy, who often keep their expensive jewelry in safes or bank vaults, sometimes hire people to wear their pearls for them so that the gems will not lose their luster.
4. Bustles which were once very popular have been out of vogue for many years.
5. Jacob met Rachel his future wife at a well.
6. Leah, Rachel's sister also became Jacob's wife.
7. Across the bay lived Mary Fiorentino the governor, and only three or four hundred yards away was the palatial home of Osgood England the soap king.
8. The brothers of Jacob's son Joseph sold him to some Midianites who in turn sold him into Egypt.
9. Sherwood Anderson's book, *Poor White,* is one of the author's strongest expressions of the recurrent theme, that industrialism has caused human frustrations never felt before.
10. Tom and his wife Daisy traveled over the world, moved from one place to another, and finally settled down in a huge mansion in East Egg which is on Long Island.

20f Use commas with sentence modifiers, conjunctive adverbs, and sentence elements out of normal word order.

Sentence modifiers like *on the other hand, for example, in fact, in the first place, I believe, in his opinion, unfortunately,* and *certainly* are set off by commas.

> Only a few poets, unfortunately, make a living by writing.
>
> Wells's early novels, I believe, stand the test of time.

Commas are frequently used with conjunctive adverbs, such as *therefore, then, consequently, nevertheless,* and *however.*

Before Clause
optional

The secretary checked the figures; therefore, the mistake was discovered.

Within Clause
optional

The secretary checked the figures; the mistake, therefore, was discovered.

Commas always separate the conjunctive adverb *however* from the rest of the sentence.

> The auditor found the error in the figures; however, the books still did not balance.
>
> The auditor found the error in the figures; the books, however, still did not balance.

Commas are not used when *however* is an adverb meaning "no matter how."

> However fast the hare ran, he could not catch the tortoise.

Use commas if necessary for clearness or emphasis when part of a sentence is out of normal order.

> Aged and infirm, the president governed through loyal ministers.

Or The president, aged and infirm, governed through loyal ministers.

But The aged and infirm president governed through loyal ministers.

20g Use commas with degrees and titles and elements in dates, places, and addresses.

Degrees and Titles	Emily Snipes, M.A., came to the reception.
	Charles Morton, Jr., Vice-Principal of Roosevelt High School, departed.
Dates	Sunday, May 31, is my birthday.
	August 1977 was very warm. OR August, 1977, was very warm. (Either is acceptable.)
	December 7, 1941, will never be forgotten. (Use commas *before* and *after*.)
	She was born 31 December 1970. (No commas are required.)
	The year 1968 was eventful. (Restrictive; no commas are required.)
Places	Cairo, Illinois, is my home town. (Use commas *before* and *after*.)
Addresses	Write the editor of *The Atlantic*, 8 Arlington Street, Boston, Massachusetts 02116. (Do not use a comma before the Zip Code.)

20h Use commas for contrast or emphasis and with short interrogative elements.

The pilot had been forced to use an auxiliary landing field, not the city airport.

The field was safe enough, wasn't it?

20i Use commas with mild interjections (words like *oh* and *ah*) and with words like *yes* and *no*.

Well, I did not think it was possible.
No, it proved to be quite simple.

20j Use commas with words in direct address and after the salutation of a personal letter.

Mary, have you seen the portrait?

Dear John,
It has been some time since I've written. . . .

20k Use commas with expressions like *he said, she remarked,* and *they replied* when used with quoted matter.

"I am planning to give up Latin," she remarked, "at the beginning of next term."

He replied, "It's all Greek to me."

20L Set off an absolute phrase with commas.

An **absolute phrase** consists of a noun followed by a modifier. It modifies the sentence as a whole, not any single element in it.

absolute phrase
Our journey over, we made camp for the night.

⟵ *absolute phrase* ⟶
The portrait having dried, the artist hung it on the wall.

20m Use commas to prevent misreading or to mark an omission.

After washing and grooming, the pup looked like a new dog.
When violently angry, elephants trumpet.
Beyond, the open fields sloped gently to the sea.

verb omitted
↓
To err is human; to forgive, divine.

20m

- *Exercise 5*

   Decide where commas need to be added in the following sentences.

   1. Inside, the convention hall resembled a huge, overcrowded barn.
   2. A few hours before she was scheduled to leave, the girl visited her father, who pleaded with her to change her mind and then finally said quietly, "Good luck."
   3. Seeing a nightingale, the American ornithologist recognized its resemblance to other members of the thrush family.
   4. Seeing a nightingale for the first time is disappointing; hearing one for the first time, unforgettable.
   5. History, one would think, ought to teach people not to make the same mistakes over again.
   6. Despite the old saying to the contrary, you can sometimes tell a book by its cover.
   7. The Vandyke beard, according to authorities, was named after Sir Anthony Van Dyck, a famous Flemish painter.
   8. Her novel is beautifully written, don't you think?
   9. While burning, cedar has a distinct and strong odor.
   10. The cloverleaf, a road arrangement that looks somewhat like a four-leaf clover, permits traffic to flow easily between two intersecting expressways.

- *Exercise 6*

   Decide where commas need to be added in the following sentences. Note: not all of the sentences are incorrect as written.

   1. The hippopotamus has a stout body, very short legs, and a large head and muzzle.
   2. Contrary to what you may have heard, the tarantula, a large hairy spider, is not highly venomous.

20m

3. Before students can understand the principles of quantum physics they must master simple algebra.

4. The large urn which was dated June 21 1900 stood in the corner of the garden and the honeysuckle vines almost hid it from view.

5. While the mystery writer was beginning work on his last novel *The Tiger's Eye* he received a note warning him not to write about anyone he knew in the Orient.

6. "The prairies are reputed to be flat" Raymond Haille a professor of geography said. "However you dwellers in the hills and mountains I tell you that there is much variety in the terrain of the prairies at some points."

7. "Yes" he continued with a little too much of the manner of a dramatic orator "Red Cloud Nebraska is a place of some geographic variety."

8. Having surprised some in his audience the speaker said "People you must develop a feeling for place must become familiar with a world about which you are uninformed."

9. Not even the presider of the meeting herself made a single contradictory statement.

10. Towers domes and stadiums provided little contrast with the overhanging clouds.

• *Exercise 7*

The authors wrote these sentences as a series of three paragraphs. Decide where commas need to be added. Note: the punctuation in some sentences is correct.

1. Sunday morning December 7 1941.

2. Clouds rushed overhead as six big aircraft carriers escorted by a pair of fast battleships three cruisers and a covey of destroyers slammed through heavy seas at twenty-four knots.

3. Their course was due south their destination a point in the ocean 275 miles north of Pearl Harbor a point close enough to launch an air strike on this main base of the U.S. Pacific Fleet.

4. Leading the left-hand column of three flattops was the veteran *Akagi* pride of the Imperial Japanese Navy.

5. Leading the right-hand column was the *Soryu* the smallest of the six at 15,900 tons displacement.

6. This task force comprised all of the first-line attack carriers of the Japanese navy.

7. It was the strongest carrier task force ever assembled.

8. Commanding the Pearl Harbor attack force was a gray-haired stoutish veteran seaman Vice-Admiral Chuichi Nagumo.

9. His only prior aviation experience had been as a light-carrier skipper in 1929.

10. Moreover he disapproved of the Pearl Harbor operation and during the planning stages had opposed it as being too risky.

11. His carriers were loaded with an antithetical combination of volatile aviation gas and high-explosive bombs and ammunition.

12. Any enemy hit short of a dud might blow one up.

13. Nevertheless Nagumo had accepted the command of the First Air Fleet and had decided to press home the attack.

14. Rear Admiral Ryunosuke Kusaka his Chief of Staff was confident that the air crews would find eight battleships in Pearl Harbor.

15. If his fliers could sink or disable the battlewagons of the U.S. Pacific Fleet he would have scored a success.

ADAPTED FROM JAMES H. BELOTE AND WILLIAM M. BELOTE,
Titans of the Seas

21

• Exercise 8

The author wrote these sentences as two paragraphs. Decide where commas need to be added. Note: the punctuation in some sentences is correct.

1. The chief deity of the Aegeans was—like that of many Asiatic cults—feminine.
2. She was the Great Goddess the Universal Mother in whom were united all the attributes and functions of divinity.
3. Above all she symbolized fertility and her influence extended over plants and animals as well as humans.
4. All the universe was her domain.
5. As celestial goddess she regulated the course of the heavenly bodies and controlled the alternating seasons.
6. On earth she caused the products of the soil to flourish gave men riches and protected them in battle and at sea she guided them on their adventurous voyages.
7. She killed or tamed fierce beasts, and she also reigned over the Underworld.
8. The Great Goddess is represented depending on the epoch either crouching or standing.
9. Sometimes she is dressed like a Cretan woman; in this case she wears a flounced skirt.
10. Her headdress varies: the hair may be free knotted with a simple fillet; it may be covered by a sort of turban decorated with flowers or aigrettes by a conical tiara in the Oriental manner or again by a very tall tiara in the shape of a topless cone.

ADAPTED FROM FELIX GUIRANDS, "Greek Mythology"

21 Unnecessary Commas

Do not use too many commas.

A comma at every pause within a sentence is not necessary.

21a Do not use a comma between subject and verb, between verb or verbal and complement, or between an adjective or an adverb and the word it modifies.

Not The guard with the drooping mustache, snapped to attention.

Not The stubborn, mischievous, child refused to respond.

A phrase set off by two commas may be used between subject and verb.

Correct The malamute, an Alaskan work dog, can survive extraordinarily cold weather.

21b Do not use a comma between two compound elements, such as verbs, subjects, complements, or predicates, except for contrast or emphasis (see **20h**).

Unnecessary He left the scene of the accident, and tried to forget that it had happened.

21c Do not use a comma before a coordinating conjunction joining two dependent clauses except for contrast or emphasis.

Unnecessary The contractor testified that the house was completed, and that the work had been done properly.

See **20a** for the use of commas to separate independent clauses.

21d Do not use a comma before *than* in a comparison or between compound conjunctions like *as . . . as, so . . . as,* and *so . . . that.*

Not John Holland was more delighted with life on the Continent, than he had thought he could be.

21h

21e Do not use a comma after *like, such as,* and similar expressions.

A comma is used before *such as* only when the phrase is non-restrictive.

> *comma here* *not here*
>   ↓   ↓
> Some languages, such as Latin and Anglo-Saxon, are still studied but no longer spoken.

21f Do not use a comma with a period, a question mark, an exclamation point, or a dash. These marks stand by themselves.

Not "Did you get the job?", her sister asked.

21g A comma may be used after a closing parenthesis but not before an opening parenthesis.

> *no comma here*
>   ↓
> When she had finished reading *The Pilgrim's Progress* (the
>
> *comma here*
>   ↓
> most popular allegory in the language), she turned next to *The House of the Seven Gables.*

21h A comma is not required after most introductory adverbial modifiers if they are short and essential or after coordinating conjunctions (see **20d**).

Optional After he had slept, he felt more confident.

   Not Thus, he passed the examination.

   Not But, some people are excessively tolerant.

21i Do not use commas to set off restrictive clauses, phrases, or appositives (see **20e**).

Not People, who live in glass houses, should not throw stones.

21j Do not use a comma between adjectives which are not coordinate (see **20c**).

Not The tired, old, work horse.

● *Exercise 9*

Identify all unnecessary commas and be prepared to explain your decisions.

1. Soccer is a popular sport in Great Britain, where it is sometimes called, football.
2. The secretary bird is so named, because, on its crest, it has feathers which resemble quill pens.
3. Restaurants, that serve excellent food at modest prices, are always popular among local people, though tourists seldom know about them.
4. After several long, expensive visits to the dentist, (especially if they are painful) people, who have always taken their teeth for granted, will probably brush more regularly.
5. "My secret of long life?", the old mountain woman said. "Why, I just do not worry about dying, like most people do."
6. Communities, near large airports, have become increasingly aware that noise pollution can be just as unpleasant as impurities in the air, or in streams.
7. The way, of celebrating certain holidays, has changed over the years, but these occasions can still be meaningful.
8. Once, huge movie houses were fashionable, but now these palaces are like dinosaurs—extinct giants, curious reminders, of the past.

9. The Olympic runner was disqualified, after she ran out of her lane, but she would not have won a gold medal, anyway.
10. The gardener vowed that he would never work for the millionaire again, and that he would go back to his small farm.

22 The Semicolon

Use a semicolon between independent clauses not joined by coordinating conjunctions *(and, but, or, nor, for, so, yet)* and between coordinate elements with internal commas.

Failure to use a semicolon between independent clauses may result in a comma splice or a fused sentence (see **2**).

22a Use a semicolon between independent clauses not connected by a coordinating conjunction.

With No Connective
For fifteen years the painting stood in the attic; even Mr. Kirk forgot it.

With a Conjunctive Adverb
In 1978 a specialist from the museum arrived and asked to examine it; then all the family became excited.

See **20f** for use of commas with conjunctive adverbs, such as *however, therefore, moreover, then, consequently,* and *nevertheless.*

With a Sentence Modifier
The painting was valuable; in fact, the museum offered five thousand dollars for it.

See **20f** for the use of commas with sentence modifiers, such as *on the other hand, for example, in fact,* and *in the first place.*

22b Use a semicolon to separate independent clauses which are long and complex or which have internal punctuation.

In many compound sentences either a semicolon or a comma may be used. The semicolon is a stronger separator than the comma.

Comma or   *Moby-Dick,* by Melville, is an adventure story, [*or;*]
Semicolon   and it is also one of the world's great philosophical novels.

Semicolon   Ishmael, the narrator, goes to sea, he says, "when-
Preferred   ever it is a damp, drizzly November" in his soul; and Ahab, the captain of the ship, goes to sea because of his obsession to hunt and kill the great albino whale, Moby Dick.

22c Use semicolons in a series between items which have internal punctuation.

The old farmer kept a variety of poultry: chickens, for eggs and Sunday dinners; turkey, for very special meals; and peacocks, for their beauty.

22d Do not use a semicolon between elements which are not coordinate.

            dependent clause   *independent*
Not   After the tugboat had signaled to the barge; it turned toward
         clause
        the wharf.

But   After the tugboat had signaled to the barge, it turned toward the wharf.

● *Exercise 10*

Identify unnecessary semicolons and commas and decide where additional ones should be inserted. Note: not all sentences are incorrect.

1. In Greek mythology Proteus was a sea god; one that could change his shape, whenever he wished.

2. The stipulations of the agreement were; that each company would keep its own name that profits would be evenly divided and that, no employees would lose their jobs; because of the merger.

3. An advanced civilization is guided by enlightened self-interest; however, it is also marked by unselfish good will.

4. The sound of the banjo drifted up from the floor below, it blended with the chatter of typewriters; and the droning of business conferences.

5. After an economic depression; people are hesitant to spend money freely; because they are afraid hard times will recur.

6. The hallway was long, and dark; and at the end of it hung an obscure painting representing a beggar; in eighteenth-century London.

7. The mutineers defeated the loyal members of the crew; took command of the ship; and locked the captain and other officers in the brig.

8. Winning is important, and rewarding; but sportsmanship is more essential in building character.

9. Fortunetelling still appeals to many people even when they realize it is superstitious nonsense; they will continue to patronize such charlatans, as palm readers.

10. The making of pottery, once a necessary craft as well as an art, has again become popular, and hundreds of young people, many of them in the country, are discovering the excitement of this form of creativity.

23 The Colon

Use a colon as a formal and emphatic mark of introduction.

23a Use a colon before quotations, statements, and series which are introduced formally.

Some of the buildings in the county are unusual: two-story antebellum homes, built mainly in the 1840's; smaller houses, which have long open hallways; and stores, some of which have two stories with porches.

A colon may be used to introduce a quotation formally when there is no verb of saying.

The warden began his short statement with a sharp reminder: "Gentlemen, you are now almost free; but some of you will not remain free for long."

23b Use a colon between two independent clauses when the second explains or amplifies the first.

> Music is more than something mechanical: it is an expression of deep feeling and ethical values.

23c Use a colon before formal appositives, including those introduced by such expressions as *namely* and *that is.*

> There are three sources of belief: reason, custom, inspiration.
>
> BLAISE PASCAL

> One element is missing from some contemporary styles: good taste.

NOTE The colon comes before *namely* and similar expressions, not after.

> After a sleepless night the senator reached his decision: namely, that he would not seek reelection.

23d Use a colon between hours and minutes to indicate time, after the salutation of a formal letter, and between city and publisher in bibliographical entries.

> 12:15 P.M.
> Dear Dr. Tyndale:
> Boston: Houghton, 1929

23e Do not use a colon after a linking verb **(10c)** or a preposition.

Faulty Some chief noisemakers are: automobiles, airplanes, and lawn mowers.

Faulty   His friend accused him of: wiggling in his seat, talking during the lecture, and not remembering what was said.

In such sentences no punctuation is needed before the series.

24 The Dash

Use a dash to introduce summaries and to indicate interruptions, informal breaks in construction, parenthetical (explanatory) remarks, and special emphasis.

In typescript a dash is made by two hyphens (--) with no space before or after.

For Summary   Attic fans, window fans, air conditioners—all were ineffective that summer.

For Sudden Interruptions   He replied, "I will consider the—No, I won't either."

For Special Emphasis   Great authors quote one book more than any other —the Bible.

25 Parentheses

Use parentheses to enclose loosely related comment or explanation and to enclose figures which number items in a series.

The oil well (the company had drilled it only as an experiment) produced a thousand barrels a day.

Harriet Tubman (1820?–1913) was an American black woman who helped many slaves escape to freedom.

The oil company refused to buy the land because (1) the owner had no clear title, (2) it was too remote, and (3) it was too expensive.

A parenthetical sentence within another sentence has no period or capital, as in the first example above. A freestanding parenthetical sentence between sentences requires parentheses, a capital, and a punctuation mark at the end.

26 Brackets

Use brackets to enlose inserted material within quotations.

> In the opinion of Arthur Miller, "There is no more reason for falling down in a faint before his [Aristotle's] *Poetics* than before Euclid's geometry."

Parentheses within parentheses are replaced by brackets ([ ]). Usually it is best to avoid a construction which calls for this intricate punctuation.

• *Exercise 11*

Decide where colons, dashes, parentheses, and brackets need to be inserted in the following sentences. Note: not all sentences are incorrect.

1. In his speech the President addressed three issues:price supports, tariffs, and our Asian policy.

2. The hiking shorts are made with an adjustable ring belt, roomy front pockets, and button-flap rear pockets.

3. The cruise it will last twenty-seven days will be from New York to Buenos Aires.

4. "And I say to you, my friends, the country is entering a period of prosperity at this point the audience cheered the like of which is rarely seen."

5. She left at 130 to visit an unusual building in the downtown area the Kennedy Building.

6. Seventy-five feet of cargo space, power disc brakes, and a four-speed transmission the new station wagon has all of these features.

7. With this camera you can get perfect exposures by following a simple procedure lining up two needles in the viewfinder and you can also take wide-angle shots very easily.

8. The scientist made a startling statement the researchers at the institute are doing hazardous studies.

9. The final score of the game was eleven to four pardon me, eleven to *three.*

10. The exhibition will visit these cities in this order 1 New York, 2 Chicago, 3 Houston, 4 Los Angeles.

27 Quotation Marks

Use quotation marks to enclose the exact words of a speaker or writer and to set off some kinds of titles.

American writers and publishers use double quotation marks (". . .") except for internal quotations (quotations within quotations), which are set off by single quotation marks ('. . .').

27a Use quotation marks to enclose direct quotations and dialogue.

Direct At one point in Shakespeare's play, Hamlet says, "To
Quotation be or not to be, that is the question. . . ."

In dialogue a new paragraph marks each change of speaker.

Dialogue "What is fool's gold?" the explorer asked.
 The geologist paused only a moment. "Really," he said, "it's pyrite, which has the color of gold."

When typing a paper, indent and single-space prose quotations which are one hundred words or longer. *Do not* use quotation marks to enclose these blocked quotations.

Poetry is single-spaced and centered between the left and right margins. The lines should be copied exactly as written.

> If you would keep your soul
> From spotted sight or sound,
> Live like the velvet mole;
> Go burrow underground.

Short quotations of poetry may be written like the regular text, not set off. Used in this way, they are put in quotation marks, and a slash (with a space before and after it) is used to indicate the line breaks in the original work.

Elinor Wylie satirically advises, "Live like the velvet mole; / Go burrow underground."

27b Use single quotation marks to enclose a quotation within a quotation.

The review explained: "Elinor Wylie is ironic when she advises, 'Live like the velvet mole.'"

27c Use quotation marks to enclose the titles of essays, articles, short stories, short poems, chapters (and other subdivisions of books or periodicals), radio and television programs, paintings, and most short musical compositions.

> D. H. Lawrence's "The Rocking-Horse Winner" is a story about the need for love.

> Chapter VII of *Walden* is entitled "The Beanfield." (For titles of books and magazines see **30a**.)

> A cheap reproduction of Mary Cassatt's "The Bath" hung on the wall above the desk.

27d Do not use quotation marks around the title of your own paper.

27e Do not use quotation marks to emphasize or change the usual meanings of words or to justify slang or attempts at humor.

Avoid   Some of the old politician's opponents were hoping that he would "kick the bucket" before the next election.

Avoid   The beggar considered himself a "rich" man.

27f Follow established conventions in positioning other marks of punctuation with quotation marks.

Periods and **commas** are placed *inside* quotation marks in American usage.

> All of the students had read "The Death of the Hired Man."
> "Amazing," the teacher said.

Semicolons and **colons** are always placed *outside* closing quotation marks.

> The customer wrote that she was "not yet ready to buy the first edition"; it was too expensive.

A **question mark** or an **exclamation point** is placed *inside* quotation marks only when the quotation itself is a direct question or an exclamation. Otherwise, these marks are placed *outside*.

> He asked, "Who is she?" (Only the quotation is a question.)
>
> "Who is she?" he asked. (Only the quotation is a question.)
>
> Did he ask, "Who is she?" (The quotation and the entire sentence are questions.)
>
> Did he say, "I know her"? (The entire sentence asks a question; the quotation makes a statement.)
>
> She shouted, "Run!" (Only the quotation is an exclamation.)
>
> How tragic that he could only say, "I'm sorry"! (The entire statement is an exclamation; the quotation is not.)

After quotations never use a comma and an exclamation point or a question mark together.

Not   "When?", I asked.
But   "When?" I asked.

Not   "Help!", I cried.
But   "Help!" I cried.

● *Exercise 12*

Decide where quotation marks need to be added in the following passage. Decide, too, where new paragraphs are necessary.

Alex Tilman, young, vigorous, and alert, walked briskly beside the little stream.   As he neared the pond, which the diligent beavers had made generations before, he thought of Thoreau's essay Walking and the sense of calm that pervaded nature.   An old man was fishing with a pole on the bank of the pond. Knowing that people who are fishing dislike noisemakers, Alex strolled quietly up to the old man and said, How's your luck today?   Oh, about like every other day, except a little worse, maybe.   Do you mean you haven't caught anything? Well, I did catch a couple of bream. But they're small, you know.   Before I left home my wife said to me, If you don't catch any sizable fish today, you might as well give it up.   And I'm beginning to wonder if she hasn't got something there. Alex watched the water for a little while, now and then stealing a glance at the unshaven man, who wore baggy breeches, a faded old flannel shirt, and a slouchy hat.   Then he dreamily said, Well, I guess most people don't really fish just for the sake of catching something.   The old gentleman looked up at him a little surprised. His eyes were much brighter and quicker than Alex had expected.   That's right, he said, but, you know, that's not the kind of wisdom you hear these days from young folks. You new around here, son?   Yes.   My wife and I just bought the old Edgewright place.   Oh.   Well, maybe you can come fishing with me sometime.   I'm usually around about this time during the day.   Alex was not eager to accept an invitation from a creature quite so shabby as this one, but he was moved by a sudden sympathy.   Yes.   Maybe.   Say, if you need any work, I might be able to find something for you to do around our place.   My wife and I are trying to get things cleaned up. A slight smile came over the old fellow's face, and he said warmly, Much obliged, but I've got more work now than I know what to do with.   So I come out here and hum Lazy Bones and fish.   On the way back to his house, Alex asked a neighbor about the old tramp who was fishing down by the pond.   Tramp! his friend repeated.   Good heavens, man, that was no tramp.   That was Angus Morgan, one of the wealthiest men in the county.

28 End Punctuation

End a declarative sentence with a period, an interrogative sentence with a question mark, and an exclamatory sentence with an exclamation point.

These marks of punctuation also have special uses within a sentence.

28a   Use a period after a sentence which makes a statement or expresses a command.

Some modern people claim to practice witchcraft.

Water the flowers.

The gardener asked whether the plant should be taken indoors in winter. (This sentence is a statement even though it expresses an indirect question.)

28b Use periods after many abbreviations.

Periods follow such abbreviations as Ms., Mr., Dr., Ave., B.C., B.A., and many others. (In British usage periods are often omitted after such abbreviations as *Mr.*)

Abbreviations of governmental and international agencies often are written without periods (FCC, TVA, UNICEF, NATO, HEW, and so forth). Usage varies. When in doubt, consult your dictionary.

A comma or another mark of punctuation may follow the period after an abbreviation, but at the end of a sentence only one period is used.

After she earned her M.A., she began studying for her Ph.D.

But if the sentence is a question or an exclamation, the end punctuation mark follows the period after the abbreviation.

When does she expect to get her Ph.D.?

28c Use three spaced periods (ellipsis points) to show an omission in a quotation.

An **ellipsis** is the omission of words in a sentence or quotation. Notice how this passage can be shortened with ellipsis points in the quotation that follows it.

Source

"He [the Indian] had no written record other than pictographs, and his conqueror was not usually interested, at the time, in writing down his thoughts and feelings for him. The stoic calm of his few reported speeches and poems gives only a hint of the rich culture that was so soon forgotten."

ROBERT E. SPILLER

28f

Quotation with Ellipsis Points

*ellipsis points not necessary
at beginning of quotation*

*one period to end sentence
and three ellipsis points*

The Indian "had no written record other than pictographs. . . .

spaces and three periods for ellipsis

The stoic calm of his . . . speeches and poems gives only a

four at end of sentence

hint of the rich culture. . . ."

28d The title of a book or a periodical has no period, but some titles may include a question mark or an exclamation point.

The Sound and the Fury   "What are Years?"
Westward Ho!   *Ah, Wilderness!*

28e Use a question mark after a direct question.

Do teachers file attendance reports?

Teachers do file attendance reports? (A question in the form of a declarative sentence.)

Question marks may follow separate questions within a single interrogative sentence.

Do you recall the time of the accident? the license numbers of the cars involved? the names of the drivers?

28f Use a question mark within parentheses to show that a date or a figure is doubtful.

Pythagoras, who died in 497 B.C. (?), was a mathematician.

NOTE   Do not use a question mark or an exclamation point within a sentence to indicate humor or sarcasm.

Not   The comedy (**?**) was a miserable failure.

28g Use an exclamation point after a word, a phrase, or a sentence to signal strong exclamatory feeling.

> Wait! I forgot my lunch!
> Stop the bus!
> What a ridiculous idea!

Use exclamation points sparingly. After mild exclamations use commas or periods.

Not   Well! I was discouraged!

But   Well, I was discouraged.

• Exercise 13

Decide where quotation marks need to be inserted or removed in the following sentences; in item 10 determine where new paragraphs should start. Decide, too, how other punctuation should be changed in the sentences.

1. "Failure is often necessary for humanity", the pastor said. Without failure, he continued, how can we retain our humility and know the full sweetness of success? For, as Emily Dickinson said, Success is counted sweetest / By those who ne'er succeed.

2. Madam, said the talent scout, I know that you think your daughter can sing, but, believe me, her voice makes the

strangest sounds I have ever heard. Mrs Audubon took her daughter "Birdie" by the hand and haughtily left the room, wondering how she could ever have been so stupid as to expose her daughter to such a "common" person?

3. Your assignment for next week, said Ms Osborn, is to read the following (to use Poe's own term) tales of ratiocination: The Purloined Letter, The Murders in the Rue Morgue, and The Mystery of Marie Roget.

4. The boy and his great-uncle were "real" friends, and the youngster listened intently when the old man spoke. Son, he would say, you can't do better than to follow the advice of Ben Franklin, who said, One today is worth two tomorrows.

5. Although she has an M A degree, the science writer referred to herself as "an unqualified . . . genetic engineer".

6. A recent report states the following: The marked increase in common stocks indicated a new sense of national security; however, the report seems to imply that this is only one of many gauges of the country's economic situation.

7. I'm over here, shouted the trapped miner to the rescue workers.

8. One of Mark Twain's most famous letters, addressed to Andrew Carnegie, reads as follows: You seem to be in prosperity. Could you lend an admirer $1.50 to buy a

hymn book with? God will bless you. I feel it; I know it. So will I . . . If there should be other applications, this one not to count".

9. In a "postscript," Mark Twain added, Don't send the hymn book; send the money; I want to make the selection myself. He signed the letter simply Mark.

10. The conversation between Aunt Hattie and the door-to-door salesman went something like this. Madam, you have been very highly recommended to us. Will you allow us to put a set of these books in your home? No. But I don't think you understand. No. What I mean is, there is no charge at all for— No. For the books themselves. No! Good day, young man.

Mechanics

29 Manuscript and Letter Form

Follow correct manuscript form in your papers and business letters.

Papers   Use white paper 8½ by 11 inches for typescript, ruled paper for longhand. Do not use onionskin. Use blue or black ink. When typing, double-space. In longhand skip every other line. Write or type on one side of the paper only. Center the title and leave extra space between title and text.

Leave ample and regular margins at the top and bottom of the page, and leave at least an inch on each side. Indent the first line of each paragraph uniformly—about one inch in longhand and five spaces in typescript.

Example of Correct Manuscript Form

Travel and Snob Appeal ⟵ *Center*

↳ *Indent 5 spaces* | ⟵ *Triple space*

     Up through the last century only the well-to-do
could afford the luxury of travel; therefore, traveling took on a kind of snob appeal. If people were
financially able to take trips abroad or even long
journeys to other parts of their own country, they
usually did so because all the best families were
doing it. Travel became a sign of affluence and culture. Wealthy young people took what used to be
called the "grand tour"--an extended trip over the
European continent--in order to complete their education. A mark of the lower classes and the uneducated
was lack of travel experience.

     As the cost of traveling came within the finan-
cial range of more and more people, they began to
overrun the favorite tourist cities of Europe.
Americans seemed almost frantic to see as much of
another part of the world as possible in a short period of time. The name of a modern motion picture
satirically expressed this frenzied activity of Americans traveling on tight schedules: If It's Tuesday,
This Must Be Belgium. So inexpensive did touring become that a book called Europe on Five Dollars a Day
became a guide for countless travelers on limited
budgets. Youths on motorcycles and even on bicycles
began to turn up in foreign cities with empty pockets
and with sleeping bags, eager to see the great places
of history.

Annotations (right margin):
- *Double-space*
- *2 spaces after periods*
- *2 hyphens and no spaces for a dash*

1 ⟵ *Page number for first*
page on bottom line (optional)

Number all pages except the first in the upper right corner. If a number is used on the first page, it should be centered at the bottom.

Before submitting any paper, read over the final draft two or three times, at least once aloud for sound. If possible, allow some time between readings. Watch especially for misspellings, typographical errors, faulty punctuation, and omissions made in revising or copying.

Revising papers after they have been read and marked by your teacher is sometimes required and always helpful.

Business letters   In writing a business letter follow the conventional form. All essential parts are included in the example on page 114. The letter should be typewritten if possible, single-spaced, with double-spacing (one blank line) between paragraphs. Paragraphs may be indented or may begin at the left margin without indentation.

Business letters are usually written on stationery 8½ by 11 inches. Fold horizontally into thirds to fit a standard-sized business envelope. For smaller envelopes fold once horizontally and then into thirds.

It is wise to determine the title and the name of the addressee, but sometimes a letter must be addressed to an organization rather than to a particular person in the organization. The once-traditional "Gentlemen" and "Dear Sir" are used less often today because they ignore the fact that the recipient may be a woman. The most conventional salutation has become "Dear Sir or Madam." However, a simplified style is recommended by the Administration Management Society; the AMS style calls for substituting a subject heading for the salutation.

● *Exercise 1*

Write a letter applying for a job. Type the letter if possible.

A Business Letter and Envelope

42 Jackson Street ⟵————— *Address of writer*
Princeton, New Jersey 08540
February 1, 1978 ⟵————— *Date*

Name and title of addressee;
6 spaces below date

Ms. Lucille M. Freeman
Director, Pine Lodge Camp
10 Commonwealth Plaza ⟵————— *Full address*
Boston, Massachusetts 02108

Dear Ms. Freeman: ⟵————— *Salutation. Use name when possible.*
⟵————— *Blank line*

    I would like to apply for a job as a counselor at
Pine Lodge Camp. I am eighteen years old and will
graduate from Princeton High School this year; I hope
to attend Douglass College in the fall. Because I
like working with children, I want to become a special
education teacher at the elementary level.

    In the summer of 1976 I was a counselor-in-train- ⟵ *Indentation pos-*
ing at Camp Lenape, Mount Pocono, Pennsylvania, where   *sible but not*
I got my Red Cross Senior Lifesaving badge and won   *necessary*
the crawl and backstroke races at the Parents' Day
swimming meet. (Ms. Mary Carter is the camp director.)
In the summer of 1977 I worked in the town recreation
program (Summerfun, 20 Nassau Street, Princeton) as a
lifeguard and swimming teacher for children nine to
twelve years old at the Madison swimming pool. My
supervisor was Mr. Luis Villa.

    If necessary, I could come to New York or Boston for
an interview. My telephone number is (609) 227-6059.

⟵————— *Blank line*
Sincerely yours, ⟵——— *Complimentary close*

Cynthia Wright

Cynthia Wright ⟵——— *Signature, handwritten*
⟵——— *Signature, typed*

Cynthia Wright
42 Jackson Street
Princeton, New Jersey 08540

Ms. Lucille M. Freeman
Director, Pine Lodge Camp
10 Commonwealth Plaza
Boston, Massachusetts 02108

30 Underlining for Italic Type

Underline to represent italics in titles of books, magazines, and newspapers and occasionally to emphasize a word or phrase.

Italic type slants *(like this).* Underline words individually (<u>like</u> <u>this</u>, not <u>like this</u>).

30a Underline titles of books (except the Bible and its divisions), periodicals, newspapers, motion pictures, television series, long musical compositions, plays, and other works published separately.

Be precise: watch initial articles *(A, An, The)* and any punctuation.

Books	<u>Adventures of Huckleberry Finn</u> <u>An American Tragedy</u>
Periodicals	<u>The Atlantic</u> <u>Smithsonian</u>
Newspapers	<u>New York Times</u>
Motion Pictures	<u>Citizen Kane</u>
Long Musical Compositions	Bizet's <u>Carmen</u> Handel's <u>Messiah</u>
Plays	<u>The Cherry Orchard</u>

30b Underline names of ships and trains.

the <u>Queen Elizabeth II</u>   the <u>U.S.S. Hornet</u>   the <u>Zephyr</u>

30c Except when they have become part of our language, underline foreign words used in an English context.

Dictionaries often give help in determining whether a word is still considered foreign or has become part of the English language. Foreign proper names should never be underlined, nor should foreign money or foreign foods that are common in the United States. Phrases are more likely to be considered foreign than are single words. Because words frequently used in the United States quickly become part of English, it is probably better not to underline a word when you are still doubtful after consulting your dictionary.

Fried grasshoppers were the *pièce de résistance* of the meal.

| | 1899 | 1902 | 1902 | 1697 | 1880 |
| | ↓ | ↓ | ↓ | ↓ | ↓ |

But The chauffeur garaged the limousine with verve and élan. (The dates show when the words [all from French] came into English, according to the *Oxford English Dictionary*. Long accepted, they are not italicized or underlined.)

30d Underline words, letters, and figures referred to as such.

The word puppy usually has delightful connotations.
Don't forget to dot your i's.

NOTE Occasionally quotation marks are used instead of underlining.

30e Avoid excessive underlining for emphasis.

Weak writing is seldom improved by mechanical tricks. Do not sprinkle a page with underlinings, dashes, or exclamation points.

30f Do not underline the title of your own paper.

● *Exercise 2*

Decide which words in the following sentences need to be underlined for italics.

1. N. Scott Momaday has written House Made of Dawn, The Way to Rainy Mountain, and The Names.
2. The manager started her speech with a quotation from the Bible and later referred to a recent story in the Los Angeles Times.
3. The Seventh Seal and The African Queen are considered classic films.
4. The soprano sang "Vissi d'arte" from Puccini's Tosca.
5. An article in Newsweek magazine has a picture of the U.S.S. Enterprise.
6. Homer's Iliad names the tribes which came to help the besieged people of Troy.
7. The new student was the presider pro tempore of the meeting.
8. The speech teacher says that my t's, d's, n's, and l's are not distinct enough.
9. Have you ever seen Tennessee Williams's play The Glass Menagerie?
10. In Ms. magazine Alice Walker reviewed Second Class Citizen, a novel of contemporary African life.

31 Spelling

Spell correctly; use a dictionary to look up words you are unsure of.

Spelling is troublesome in English because many words are not spelled as they sound *(laughter, slaughter);* because some distinct pairs and triplets sound the same *(capital, capitol; there, they're, their; to, too, two);* and because many words are pronounced with the vowel sound "uh," which gives no clue to spelling (sensible, capable, science).

31

Many misspellings are due to the omission of syllables in habitual mispronunciations *(accident-ly* for *acciden-tal-ly);* the addition of syllables *(disas-ter-ous* for *disas-trous);* or the changing of syllables *(prespiration* for *perspiration).*

There are no infallible guides to spelling in English, but the following are helpful.

ie or ei?

> Use *i* before *e*
> Except after *c*
> Or when sounded as *a*
> As in *neighbor* and *weigh.*

Words with ie: believe, chief, field, grief, piece
Words with ei *after* c: receive, receipt, ceiling, deceit, conceive
Words with ei *sounded as* a: freight, vein, reign
Exceptions to memorize: either, neither, leisure, seize, weird, height

Drop final silent e?

Drop the *e* when a suffix (word ending) begins with a vowel.

curse, cursing; come, coming; pursue, pursuing; arrange, arranging; dine, dining

Typical exceptions: courageous, noticeable, dyeing (compare *dying*), singeing (compare *singing*)

Keep the *e* when a suffix begins with a consonant.

live, lively; nine, ninety; hope, hopeful; love, loveless; arrange, arrangement

Typical exceptions: awful, ninth, truly, argument

Change y *to* i?

Change *y* to *i* when the *y* is preceded by a consonant.

> gully, gullies; try, tried; fly, flies; apply, applied; party, parties

Do not change *y* to *i* when the *y* is preceded by a vowel.

> valley, valleys; attorney, attorneys; convey, conveyed; pay, pays; deploy, deploys.

Do not change *y* to *i* when adding -*ing*.

> try, trying; fly, flying; apply, applying

Double final consonant?

If the suffix begins with a consonant, do not double the final consonant of the base word: *man, manly.*

If the suffix begins with a vowel, double the final consonant when it is preceded by a single vowel.

> *Monosyllables:* pen, penned; blot, blotted; sit, sitting

> *Polysyllables accented on the last syllable:* defer, deferring; begin, beginning; omit, omitting; occur, occurring

If the suffix begins with a vowel, do not double the final consonant when it is preceded by two vowels.

> despair, despairing; leer, leering

If the suffix begins with a vowel, do not double the final consonant when it is one of a pair of final consonants preceded by a single vowel.

> jump, jumping; work, working

If the suffix begins with a vowel, do not double the final consonant if the word is polysyllabic and the syllable preceding the suffix is unaccented after the addition of the suffix.

> defer, deference; prefer, preference; develop, developing; labor, labored

31

Add s or es?

Add *s* for plurals of most nouns.

girl, girls; book, books

Add *es* when the plural has an extra syllable.

church, churches; fox, foxes

Add *s* to nouns ending in *o* preceded by a vowel.

radio, radios; cameo, cameos

Usually add *es* to nouns ending in *o* preceded by a consonant. Consult your dictionary when in doubt.

potatoes, heroes

But cargoes or cargos; flamingos or flamingoes

NOTE The plurals of proper names are generally formed by adding *s* or *es*.

Darby, the Darbys; Delano, the Delanos; Jones, the Joneses

• Exercise 3

Choose the correctly spelled word in each pair. Use a dictionary as needed.

1. siege, seige
2. weird, wierd
3. relieve, releive
4. lovly, lovely
5. comeing, coming
6. arranging, arrangeing
7. changable, changeable
8. trys, tries
9. couragous, courageous
10. nineth, ninth
11. valleys, vallies
12. alloted, allotted
13. runing, running
14. steering, steerring
15. patrolling, patroling
16. boxs, boxes
17. latches, latchs
18. solos, soloes
19. the Ruizes, the Ruiz's
20. the Kellies, the Kellys

31

• *Exercise 4*

According to a newspaper article, the twenty most commonly misspelled words are the following. Choose the correct spelling of each, using a dictionary as needed.

1. battalion, battallion
2. coolly, cooly
3. desiccate, desicate
4. disservice, diservice
5. disippate, dissipate
6. embarrass, embarass
7. Filipino, Fillippino
8. friccasee, fricassee
9. harrass, harass
10. hypocrisy, hypocricy
11. inoculate, innoculate
12. knicknack, knickknack
13. loneliness, lonliness
14. liquify, liquefy
15. mayonaise, mayonnaise
16. medallion, medalion
17. moccasin, mocasin
18. parrafin, paraffin
19. sacriligious, sacrilegious
20. supercede, supersede

Other Words Frequently Misspelled

absence	arctic	cemetery
accidentally	argument	changeable
accommodate	arithmetic	changing
accumulate	ascend	choose
acknowledgment	athletic	chose
acquaintance	attendance	coming
acquitted	balance	commission
advice	beginning	committee
advise	believe	comparative
amateur	benefited	compelled
analysis	bouillon	conceivable
analyze	boundaries	conferred
annual	Britain	conscience
apartment	business	conscientious
apparatus	calendar	control
apparent	candidate	criticize
appearance	category	deferred

31

definite
description
desperate
dictionary
dining
disappearance
disappoint
disastrous
discipline
dissatisfied
dormitory
ecstasy
eighth
eligible
eliminate
eminent
encouraging
environment
equipped
especially
exaggerate
excellence
exhilarate
existence
experience
explanation
familiar
fascinate
February
fiery
foreign
formerly
forty
fourth
frantically
fulfill

generally
government
grammar
grandeur
grievous
guerrilla
height
hemorrhage
heroes
hindrance
hoping
humorous
hypocrite
immediately
incidentally
incredible
independence
inevitable
intellectual
intelligence
interesting
irrelevant
irresistible
judgment
knowledge
laboratory
laid
led
liaison
lightning
maintenance
maneuver
manufacture
marshal
mathematics
may

maybe
miniature
minuscule
mischievous
mysterious
necessary
nickel
niece
ninety
noticeable
occasionally
occurred
omitted
opportunity
optimistic
parallel
paralyze
pastime
performance
permissible
perseverance
personnel
perspiration
physical
picnicking
possibility
practically
precede
precedence
preference
preferred
prejudice
preparation
prevalent
privilege
professor

pronunciation	schedule	temperamental
prophecy	scurrilous	tendency
prophesy	secretary	their
probably	seize	thorough
quantity	separate	to
quiet	sergeant	too
quite	severely	tragedy
quizzes	shining	tries
recede	siege	truly
receive	similar	tyranny
recognize	skillful	unanimous
recommend	sophomore	undoubtedly
reference	specifically	until
referred	specimen	usually
repetition	stationary	vilify
resistance	stationery	village
restaurant	statue	villain
rhythm	succeed	weather
ridiculous	successful	weird
sacrifice	surprise	whether
salary	studying	writing

32 Hyphenation and Syllabication

Use a hyphen in certain compound words and in words divided at the end of a line.

32a Consult a dictionary to determine whether a compound is hyphenated or written as one or more words.

Hyphenated	One Word	Two or More Words
one-way	highway	right of way
white-hot	whitewash	white heat
water-cool	watermelon	water system

32b

32b Hyphenate a compound of two or more words used as a single modifier before a noun.

Hyphen	**No Hyphen After Noun**
She is a *well-known* executive	The executive is *well known.*

A hyphen is not used when the first word of such a group is an adverb ending in -*ly.*

Hyphen	**No Hyphen**
a *half-finished* task	a *partly finished* task

32c Hyphenate spelled-out compound numbers from *twenty-one* through *ninety-nine.*

32d Follow accepted syllabication in hyphenating a word at the end of a line.

When in doubt, consult a dictionary. Hyphenate only between syllables, and place the hyphen only at the end of the first line, not at the beginning of the next.

Do not divide monosyllables even if they are long *(thought, strength, cheese),* and do not set off a single letter *(a-bout, might-y).* Prefixes and suffixes may be set off, though it is preferable not to carry over a two-letter suffix *(straight-ened,* not *straighten-ed.)* Compounds normally written with a hyphen *(self-satisfied)* should not be divided elsewhere at the end of a line (not *self-satis-fied).*

● *Exercise 5*

Choose the correct spelling of each of the following compounds. Use a dictionary as needed.

1. able bodied, able-bodied
2. poorly informed, poorly-informed

33

3. deepseated, deep-seated
4. thirty five, thirty-five
5. nonfiction, non-fiction
6. eight hundred, eight-hundred
7. lighthearted, light-hearted
8. goodlooking, good-looking
9. wishy washy, wishy-washy
10. seventyseven, seventy-seven
11. badly needed, badly-needed
12. self confidence, self-confidence
13. darkroom, dark-room
14. headache, head-ache
15. spoonful, spoon-ful
16. high pitched, high-pitched
17. highlight, high-light
18. mother in law, mother-in-law
19. hardboiled, hard-boiled
20. newly found, newly-found

33 The Apostrophe

Use the apostrophe to form the possessive case of many nouns, to form contractions, to show omissions, and to indicate some plurals.

Use **'s** to form the possessive of singular nouns.

> child**'s**, man**'s**, deer**'s**, lady**'s**, mother-in law**'s**
> Charles**'s**, Watts**'s**, Dickens**'s**, waitress**'s**

NOTE   Some writers use only the apostrophe to form the possessive of singular nouns ending in *s;* the trend is away from this usage, however.

Use **'** without *s* to form the possessive of plural nouns ending in *s.*

> the Joneses' car, the Dickenses' home, the waitresses' tips

Use **'s** to form the possessive of plural nouns not ending in *s*.

children**'s**, men**'s**

Use **'s** to form the possessive of indefinite pronouns.

anybody**'s**, everyone**'s**, somebody else**'s**, neither**'s**

NOTE Do not use an apostrophe with personal pronouns like *his, hers, theirs, ours,* and *its* (meaning "of it"). *It's* means "it is."

Use **'s** with only the last noun for joint possession in a pair or a series.

Marge and Jack**'s** bicycle (The two jointly own one bicycle.)
Marge**'s** and Jack**'s** bicycles (Each owns a bicycle.)

Use **'** to show omissions or to form contractions.

the roaring '20s, o'clock, jack-o'-lantern, we'll, don't, can't, it's (meaning "it is")

Use **'s** to form the plural of numerals, letters, and words referred to as words.

three 7**'s** (*but* three sevens), four *a***'s**, six *the***'s**

• *Exercise 6*

Choose the correct form in each pair below.

1. women's clothing, womens clothing
2. children's clothing, childrens clothing
3. Carlos' book, Carlos's book
4. the Bower's house, the Bowerses' house
5. the Martinez' party, the Martinezes' party
6. nobody's business, nobodys business
7. someone's notebook, someones' notebook
8. coat of her's, coat of hers
9. it's fur collar, its fur collar

34

10. Sherry and Joan's room, Sherry's and Joan's room
11. ten oclock, ten o'clock
12. doesn't, doesnt
13. It's William, Its William
14. shouldnt, shouldn't
15. two *I*'s, two *I*s

34 Capital Letters

Use a capital letter to begin a sentence and to mark a proper noun—the name of a particular person, place, or thing.

Capitalize the first word of a sentence, the pronoun *I,* and the interjection *O.*

Capitalize first, last, and important words in titles, including the second part of hyphenated words.

> *Across the River and into the Trees*
> "The Man Against the Sky"
> "After Apple-Picking"

NOTE Articles *(a, an, the),* short prepositions, and conjunctions are not capitalized unless they begin or end a title.

Capitalize first words of direct quotations and words capitalized by the author.

> Carlyle said, "Meanwhile, we will hate Anarchy as Death, which it is. . . ."

Capitalize titles preceding a name.

> Mayor White

Capitalize the word *president* when it refers to the President of the United States.

> The President is not expected to veto the measure.

NOTE Do not capitalize other titles that name an office or a rank when they are used alone.

> The stockholders sat down, and the president called for order.
> A lieutenant deserves a good living allowance.

Capitalize degrees and titles after a name.

> Jeffrey E. Tyndale, Sr., Ph.D., J.D.
> Abraham Lincoln, Attorney at Law

NOTE Do not capitalize names of occupations used as appositives (explanatory words or phrases) or as descriptions.

> Abraham Lincoln, a young lawyer from Springfield, took the case.

Capitalize words of family relationship used as names when not preceded by a possessive pronoun.

> After Father died, Mother carried on the business.

But After my father died, my mother carried on the business.

Capitalize proper nouns and some of their derivatives.

	But
Queen Victoria, Victorian	pasteurize
Venice, Venetian blind	a set of china
the West, a Westerner	west of the river
Clifton Street	my street
the Mississippi River	the Mississippi and Ohio rivers

Capitalize months, days of the week, and holidays.

> April, Friday, the Fourth of July, Labor Day

NOTE   Do not capitalize seasons and numbered days of the month unless they name holidays.

> spring, the third of July

Capitalize historical events.

> the Reformation
> the Civil War

NOTE   Do not capitalize centuries.

> the twentieth century . .

Capitalize B.C., A.D., words designating the Deity, religious denominations, and sacred books.

> in 273 B.C.
> our Creator, the Trinity, Yahweh, Allah, Buddha, Jesus
> Catholic, Protestant, Jewish
> the Bible, the Koran

• *Exercise 7*

Decide which words in the following sentences need to be capitalized.

1. like the ballads of england and scotland, polynesian oral verse exists in more than one version.
2. the title of the article i read was "a graduate's tribute to dad."
3. the police sergeant arrested a man who turned out to be a city councilor.
4. this summer the fourth of july comes on a monday.
5. the last punic war took place from 149 to 146 b.c.
6. yesterday aunt debbie took us to a baptist picnic.
7. the declaration of independence begins, "when in the course of human events. . . ."
8. i have not read much literature of nineteenth-century america.

9. the return address on the envelope was that of jean simmons, m.d.
10. the blenheim pharmacy is on jefferson street.

35 Abbreviations

Avoid most abbreviations in formal writing.

Abbreviations are short cuts. A few are accepted in all kinds of writing; most are not. The following are acceptable in any context.

Use abbreviations before names.

> Mr., Mrs., Ms., Dr., St. *or* Ste. (for *Saint,* not *Street*), Rev. (but only with a first name: Rev. Ernest Jones, not Rev. Jones)

Use abbreviations after names.

> M.D. (and other degrees), Jr., Sr., Esq.

Use abbreviations in footnotes and bibliographies. See **48.**

> ed., pp.

Use abbreviations for some agencies and organizations.

> TVA, NAACP, FBI

Use abbreviations with dates and time.

> B.C. and A.D. (with dates expressed in numerals, as 500 B.C.)
> A.M. and P.M. or a.m. and p.m. (with hours expressed in numerals, as 4:00 A.M.)

Spell out names of days, months, units of measurement, and (except in addresses) states and countries.

> Friday (*not* Fri.)
> February (*not* Feb.)
> pounds (*not* lbs)
> Sauk Center, Minnesota (*not* Minn.)
> *Exception:* Washington, D.C.

36 Numbers

Spell out numbers that can be written in one or two words.

twenty-three
one thousand

Use figures for other numbers.

123
1 $^{13}/_{16}$
$1,001.00

NOTE Newspapers and government publications generally use figures for numbers above ten.

Spell out numbers at the beginning of a sentence. If the spelled-out amount is awkward, recast the sentence.

Use numerals for figures in a series and for tabulations and statistics:

One polar bear weighed 200 pounds; another, 526; the third, 534.

Use figures for dates, street numbers, page references, percentages, and numbers used with abbreviations.

Use Figures	**Spell Out**
July 3, 1776 (*not* 3rd)	the third of July
1010 State Street	Fifth Avenue
See page 50.	The book has fifty pages.
He paid 8 per cent interest.	
The concert begins at 6 P.M.	The concert begins at six o'clock.
(*or* 6:00 P.M.)	

36

- *Exercise 8*

  In the following sentences decide where abbreviations are and are not permissible; decide, too, where numbers should be written as figures and where they must be spelled out.

  1. Doctor Smithers and Reverend Ernest Martin attended the reception.
  2. We leave for San Juan, P.R., on Fri., Feb. third.
  3. A hundred and forty-five people—forty-two women, forty one men, and sixty-two children—were in the group.
  4. The movie is shown at seven-thirty and nine-thirty P.M.
  5. According to page sixty-two of today's paper $46,000 is the asking price of the house.
  6. The benefit raised five thousand and five dollars for the local hospital.
  7. She lives at eighty-seven Madison St.
  8. That year the NAACP held its annual convention in Saint Louis.
  9. The annual rate of interest on a revolving charge account can be as much as eighteen per cent.
  10. We will leave for home on July 5th.

Diction and Style

37 Standard English and Style

Use Standard English except in special situations, and consult your dictionary on questions of usage. Use a style appropriate to your subject.

The language in generally accepted use in the English-speaking countries is known as **Standard English.** It may be characterized as the language of educated persons. Though it varies in some details from one country to another, as is indicated by such labels as *British* in dictionaries, it is the common language of the great majority of those who communicate in English, and that is why it is taught in schools and colleges. **Nonstandard,** correspondingly, refers to words, usages, spellings, or pronunciations not usually found in the speech or writing of educated persons.

    Diction is the choice and use of words. Consult your dictionary for definitions of the status or usage labels it employs—for example, *Nonstandard, Informal, Slang, Vulgar, Obsolete, Archaic, Rare, Poetic,* and *Regional.* **Informal,** or colloquial, language, which is appropriate in certain situations (though usually not in English papers), does not include regional language, or dialect, which has a separate dictionary label. The best sources of information are dictionaries which record both current and past usage. **Archaic** is the label given to words that were commonly used at one time but are now rare and generally identified with an older style of language.

A dictionary describes usage; it employs labels and lets you make your own choices. In minor matters dictionaries do not always agree. For a given word dictionaries may offer more than one acceptable form; for example, in more than one current dictionary you will find the forms *cooperate, co-operate,* and *coöperate.*

Particularly useful for students are the following desk dictionaries:

The American Heritage Dictionary of the English Language, High School Edition. Boston: Houghton Mifflin Company.

The Random House College Dictionary. New York: Random House.

Webster's New Collegiate Dictionary. Springfield, Mass.: G & C. Merriam.

Webster's New World Dictionary of the American Language. Cleveland: Collins-World Publishing Company.

Diction is choice of words; **style** is manner of writing, the way writers express their thoughts in language. Effective writing always involves the choice of words and expressions, the arrangement of words in sentences, and variety in the patterns of sentences. Sentences which express similar ideas may have vastly different effects, and much of the difference is a matter of style. Writing may be whimsical, poetic, terse, flippant, imaginative, literal, and so on. Develop the habit of noticing the style and tone of what you read and what you write. Your style should be appropriate to your subject and to your personality.

37a Use slang only when nothing else will serve as well.

Slang is a colorful nonstandard language usually invented by special groups. The main objection to slang is that it is too often an easy, popular rubber stamp which only approximates exact thought. A person who said, "He's a jerk" would not communicate much. What precisely does this mean except that the person referred to is in some vague and unspecified way unattractive?

Another objection to slang in student papers is that it may turn out to be unintentionally funny. Slang expressions are particularly out of place in a context that is otherwise dignified:

> The violin virtuoso's performance on the cello was a *real bomb.*
> When Macbeth recoiled at the thought of murder, Lady Macbeth urged him not to *chicken out.*

Slang which is vivid and useful sometimes becomes Standard English. *Skyscraper, bus,* and *mob* were once slang; and because no other word was found to convey quite the same meanings as *date,* it is no longer slang.

37b Use dialect only in situations where it is appropriate.

The words, usages, and linguistic patterns typical of one section of the country or of a particular group are often termed **dialect.** Dialectal characteristics are a cultural heritage and a continuing source of richness, flavor, and variety. They can be used in writing to give the authenticity of local or particular speech. In general or formal communication it is usually wise to use Standard English, which is understood by all English speakers.

● *Exercise 1*

Select ten of the following expressions and identify each with an appropriate label—Standard, Nonstandard, Informal, Slang, and so on. There is no universal system of usage labels. Read the preliminary pages in your dictionary, and be sure you understand its particular system. Use your dictionary and your own judgment.

ain't

beak (nose)

blockhead

bunk (nonsense)

drag race

exam

freak out

fresh (presumptuous)

ghetto

gobbledygook

goober

greenhorn

high-hat

kid (child)

kine (cows)

loco (insane)

loser (a failure)

mad (angry)

mayhap

off-the-record

pad (apartment)

peekaboo

pep

rattle (to confuse)

shades (sunglasses)

shipshape

sidle

steed

TV

zany

37c Avoid improprieties. Use words in their correct functions and meanings.

An **impropriety** is an unacceptable usage in speech or writing. It is a Standard English word which is misused by being given the wrong function or the wrong meaning in a particular context.

A **functional impropriety** is the use of a word as the wrong part of speech. A noun, for example, should not serve as an adjective or verb if there is a related adjective or verb form that is correct. Thus it is not Standard English to write *orchestra selection* for *orchestral selection* or *selection by the orchestra*.

The wrong meaning for a word can also be an impropriety. See **37g**.

The following list contains examples of the most common kinds of functional improprieties. Those that dictionaries list in this sense are described by several usage labels. *Invite* is sometimes described as informal or as dialect, *suspicioned* as nonstandard, and *eats* as slang. All should be avoided in writing.

Improprieties	**Proper Forms**
psychology approach (noun for adjective)	*psychological* approach
suspicioned (noun made into verb)	*suspected*
an *invite* (verb for noun)	an *invitation*
good *eats* (verb for noun)	good *eating,* good *food*
stagnate waters (verb for adjective)	*stagnant* waters
surprising great number (adjective for adverb)	*surprisingly* great number

37d Use correct idioms.

An **idiom** is a proper language habit, the right way to join together a group of associated words. Separated, the words do not suggest the meaning of the idiom. Such expressions as *run for office* or *down and out* cannot be understood literally. A wrong word in an idiomatic expression causes an error in meaning or awkwardness. Many English idioms are verb phrases—for example, *put on, put out, put out about* (or *by*), *put up, put in, put down. Differ from* means "to be unlike"; *differ with* means "to disagree with." Many common errors in English idiom occur in the use of prepositions after verbs or other parts of speech. A good dictionary lists idiomatic uses of all kinds.

Study the following list of common idioms.

Idiomatic	**Unidiomatic**
according to	according with
capable of	capable to
conform to (*or* with)	conform in
die of	die from
every now and then	ever now and then
except for	excepting for
identical with	identical to
in accordance with	in accordance to
incapable of doing	incapable to do
in search of	in search for
intend to do	intend on doing
in 1980	in the year of 1980
off	off of
on the whole	on a whole
plan to	plan on
prior to	prior than
similar to	similar with
superior to	superior than
try to see	try and see
type of	type of a

● *Exercise 2*

Decide which idiom in each pair is correct. Use a dictionary as needed.

1. accede to, accede with
2. inferior from, inferior to

3. abide by, abide for
4. agree for, agree to
5. oblivious of, oblivious about
6. every so often, ever so often
7. (in the sense of "await") wait for, wait on
8. providing that, provided that
9. (verb) contrast with, contrast to
10. kind of a, kind of

37e Avoid specialized vocabulary in writing for the general reader.

All specialists from cook to engineer to philosopher have their own vocabularies. Some technical words find their way into general use; most do not. We know the plastic *Lucite,* but not its chemical name, the acrylic resin *polymethyl methacrylate.*

Trouble comes when specialists either cannot or do not see the need to express their ideas in language for the general reader. The following passage, for instance, should not be addressed to a general group or a wide audience.

> The neonate's environment consists in primitively contrasted perceptual fields weak and strong: loud noises, bright lights, smooth surfaces, compared with silence, darkness and roughness. The behavior of the neonate has to be accounted for chiefly by inherited motor connections between receptors and effectors. There is at this stage, in addition to the autonomic nervous system, only the sensorimotor system to call on. And so the ability of the infant to discriminate is exceedingly low. But by receiving and sorting random data through the identification of recurrent regularity, he does begin to improve reception. Hence he can surrender the more easily to single motivations, ego-involvement in satisfactions.
>
> JAMES K. FEIBLEMAN, *The Stages of Human Life*

Contrast the foregoing passage with the following, which is on the same general subject of the infant but which is written so that the general reader—not just a specialized few—can understand it.

> Research clearly indicates that an infant's senses are functional at birth. He experiences the whack from the doctor. He is sensitive to pressure, to changes in temperature, and to pain, and he responds specifically to these stimuli. . . . How about sight? Research on infants 4–8 weeks of age shows that they can see about as well as adults. . . . The difference is that the infant cannot make sense out of what he sees. Nevertheless, what he sees does register, and he begins to take in visual information at birth. . . . In summary, the neonate (an infant less than a month old) is sensitive not only to internal but also to external stimuli. Although he cannot respond adequately, he does take in and process information.
>
> IRA J. GORDON, *Human Development: From Birth Through Adolescence*

The only technical term in the passage is *neonate;* and unlike the writer of the first passage, who also uses the word, the second author defines it for the general reader. Special vocabularies may obscure meaning. Moreover, they tempt the writer into the use of inflated and vague words instead of plain ones—a style sometimes known as *gobbledygook* or *governmentese* because it flourishes in bureaucratic writing. Harry S. Truman made a famous statement about the presidency: "The buck stops here." This straightforward assertion might be written by some bureaucrats as follows: "It is incumbent upon the President of the United States of America to uphold the responsibility placed upon him by his constituents to exercise the final decision-making power."

37f Avoid overused expressions. Strive for fresh and original phrases.

Clichés are stock phrases and figures of speech once striking but used so often that they have lost their freshness and are now trite. *Burn the midnight oil* once evoked an image, but it has been used so many times that we no longer visualize the person toiling by lamplight. Examples of triteness are innumerable: *it is interesting to note, all too soon, pandemonium reigned, apple of his (her) eye, tired but happy, quick as a flash, few and far between, such is life,* and so forth.

37g Be exact. Use words in their precise meanings.

Knowledge of idiom, use of a dictionary, and awareness of the ways words are used—all these are necessary for precision in writing. Correct use of words usually derives from good habits with language rather than from rules. The misused words in the following sentences express wrong meanings.

> She was *overtaken* by the heat. (*Overcome* was intended.)
> *Foremost,* both librarians lost their patience. (Was *Most important* or *First* intended?)
> She *parallels* the love she feels with the permanence of a tree. (*Compares . . . to* would be better.)

Misuse of one word for another that is somewhat like it can make a sentence ridiculous. (See **37c.**)

> Her dishonesty hurt her *conscious.* (The word is *conscience.*)
> Hamlet wished to get *avenge* for the murder of his father. *(revenge)*
> As the sun beams down upon the swamp, no different varieties of color are reflected—only the unreal grayish color of dead *vegetarian. (vegetation)*

Other examples are *climatic* and *climactic, statue* and *statute* or *stature, instance* and *incident,* and *affect* and *effect.* Nonwords should never be used: for example, *interpretate* for *interpret.* Nor should nonstandard forms be used for standard forms: *irregardless* for *regardless.*

● *Exercise 3*

Identify the clichés and incorrect, inexact, or misused words and expressions in the following sentences.

1. It goes without saying that the value of a college education cannot be measured in money, but when all is said and done, it is possible to compute how much a college diploma is worth to the average graduate.
2. The meal was fabulous, and the service was fantastic.
3. The girl wanted to marry a strong, silent type, and at long last she tied the knot with a man who was quiet as a mouse.
4. Holidays always repress some people.
5. On the outskirts of the small town a sign was erected that renounced that this was the home of the one and only Fitz Fitzsimmons.
6. After eight days on a life raft the survivor was weak as a kitten, but his overall condition was unbelievable.
7. The brothers were as different as night and day, but each was fit as a fiddle.
8. The attorney jumped to her feet and said, "That is irrevalent and immaterial."
9. At the retirement dinner the corporation president toasted the janitor and told him that his daily presents in the building would be sorely missed.
10. The farmer recalled those mornings as cold as ice when the ground was hard as a rock and when he shook like a leaf as he arose at the crack of dawn.

● *Exercise 4*

In the following passage select from the alternatives in parentheses the word or phrase which you think the author used. The choices involve exactness in meaning, idiom,

37g

triteness or originality, level of diction, and just plain good taste. Be prepared to defend your choices.

Shakespeare, who thought *(a lot, a great deal, a whole lot)* about the relations of fathers and children, makes this problem the subject of several of his best plays. He shows us a father who, with vast dexterity and *(push, ginger, vinegar, energy)*, has won himself a *(good job, great position)*. The *(dad, father)* loves his *(progeny, son)*, and hopes that he will share the *(loot, rewards)* and *(responsibilities, love)* of power. The *(kid, brat, son)* is *(really together, talented)* and *(cute, charming, sweet)*, brave and *(peppy, energetic, pushy)*. It would be *(easy, a pushover)*, one would think, and *(fun, pleasant)* for him to *(throw in with, amalgamate with, join)* his *(sire, old man, father)*. *(There's, There is)* no compulsion. He may sit at home playing shove-ha'penny if he *(selects, chooses);* or hunt all week during the season; or *(diddle around, waste time harmlessly)* in other ways. But he chooses to become a gangster. He is only an amateur, but he is on the fringe of the *(pro, professional)* crooks. His best *(chum, friend, pal)* is a broken-down old *(villain, ruffian, codger)* who has drunk *(most, almost)* all his gifts *(away, down, up)* and is living *(by, off of)* the remainder of his *(head, wits)*. Hal sees far more of Falstaff than he does *(of, with)* his father, King Henry IV. He makes Falstaff into a *(sort of, sort of a) (substitute, second-string)* father, laughing with him as he *(can't, cannot)* with his father. As the play goes on, it is *(harder and harder, tougher and tougher)* to understand *(what's, what is)* wrong with Hal. Why should he throw away his chances? Why does he want to hurt his father? He *says* he is doing it so that he can get more praise for reforming later; but that is not the real reason, and it never comes up after his *(reform, going straight)* takes place. The real reason *(appears, shows up)* when his father is in genuine danger and when Hal himself is challenged by a rival of his own age. Then he rushes to help the king's cause, and kills his challenger, Hotspur.   Adapted from GILBERT HIGHET, *The Art of Teaching*

37h   Add new words to your vocabulary.

Good writers have large storehouses of words, and they know the precise ones they need to express their meanings.

Your vocabulary reflects your individuality, your education, and some aspects of your various abilities. In reading, pay careful attention to words you have never seen before. Look them up in a dictionary. Write them down if you need to. Remember them. Recognize them the next time you see them, and learn to use them. Your knowledge of words not only determines your vocabulary but also affects your abilities as a thinker and a writer.

- *Exercise 5*

Vocabulary Test: Decide which word or phrase is nearest in meaning to each key word. Then check yourself by using a dictionary. Notice that Exercise 5 consists entirely of monosyllables and that Exercise 6 contains words of more than one syllable. (Adapted from It Pays to Increase Your Word Power, *by Peter Funk)*

1. vie (vī): (a) to covet, (b) compete, (c) stimulate, (d) surpass
2. eke (ēk): (a) to dilute, (b) supplement, (c) coax, (d) revive
3. brunt (brŭnt): (a) abrupt, (b) impact, (c) insult, (d) malice
4. sloth (slōth, slôth, slŏth): (a) clumsiness, (b) sadness, (c) stupidity, (d) idleness
5. cull (kŭl): (a) to win over, (b) till, (c) select, (d) memorize
6. qualm (kwäm, kwôm): (a) warmth, (b) misgiving, (c) duty, (d) peace
7. moot (mo̅o̅t): (a) gloomy, (b) ugly, (c) debatable, (d) spiritless

8. bane (bān): (a) banter, (b) mystery, (c) affliction, (d) exile
9. deign (dān): (a) to condescend, (b) pretend, (c) disparage, (d) refuse
10. tryst (trĭst): (a) appointment, (b) coyness, (c) faith, (d) ruse
11. irk (ûrk): (a) to scold, (b) make a wry face, (c) urge, (d) annoy
12. drone (drōn): (a) to talk monotonously, (b) complain, (c) be idle, (d) stretch
13. mere (mîr): (a) nothing but, (b) humble, (c) only one, (d) weak
14. deem (dēm): (a) to consider, (b) speculate, (c) acknowledge, (d) consent
15. loll (lŏl): (a) to cuddle, (b) flatter, (c) lounge, (d) soothe or quiet

• Exercise 6

Vocabulary Test: Decide which word or phrase is nearest in meaning to each key word. Then check yourself by using a dictionary. (Adapted from It Pays to Increase Your Word Power, *by Peter Funk)*

1. semantics (sə·măn′tĭks): (a) study of word meanings, (b) science of sounds, (c) sleight of hand, (d) origin of words
2. fiat (fī′ăt, fē′ät): (a) power, (b) contradiction, (c) command, (d) end
3. platitude (plăt′ə·tōōd′, plăt′ə·tyōōd′): (a) rule of life, (b) wise saying, (c) flat surface, (d) trite remark
4. nomadic (nō·măd′ĭk): (a) adventuresome, (b) fixed, (c) romantic, (d) roaming
5. hurtle (hûrt′l): (a) to throw away, (b) jump over, (c) trip, (d) rush headlong

6. punitive (pyōō′nə·tĭv): (a) pertaining to punishment, (b) insignificant, (c) stimulating, (d) repulsive

7. cavil (kăv′əl): (a) to make fun of, (b) find fault, (c) insult, (d) whine

8. heinous (hā′nəs): (a) insulting, (b) ugly, (c) wicked, (d) dark

9. augment (ôg·mĕnt′): (a) to increase, (b) urge, (c) lose, (d) dispute

10. insidious (ĭn·sĭd′ē·əs): (a) of doubtful origin, (b) secret, (c) serious, (d) treacherous

11. exonerate (ĕg·zŏn′ə·rāt′): (a) to praise, (b) absolve, (c) elevate, (d) daydream

12. inure (ĭn·yoŏr′): (a) to hurt, (b) accustom, (c) deprive, (d) confine

13. complicity (kəm·plĭs′ə·tē): (a) sharing in wrongdoing, (b) calmness, (c) state of well-being, (d) clarity

14. obtuse (ŏb·toōs′, ŏb·tyoōs′): (a) stubborn, (b) profound, (c) stupid, (d) blunt in manner.

15. mawkish (môk′ĭsh): (a) obstinate, (b) clumsy, (c) dumb, (d) sentimental

38 Wordiness

Omit needless words and irrelevant ideas.

Conciseness gives force to writing. Do not pad your paper with words merely to complete an assignment.

Use one word for many.

The love letter was written by somebody who did not sign a name. (13 words)

The love letter was anonymous (*or* was not signed). (5 or 6 words)

38

Use the active voice for conciseness (see **5**).

The truck was overloaded by the workers. (7 words)
The workers overloaded the truck. (5 words)

Revise sentence structure for conciseness.

Another element which adds to the effectiveness of a speech
is its emotional content. (14 words)

Emotional content also makes a speech more effective. (8
words)

When possible, avoid constructions with *It is* and *There are*.

Not It is truth which will prevail.
But Truth will prevail.

Use one word, not two with the same meaning (tautology).

Basic and fundamental principles. (4 words)
Basic principles. (2 words)

Study your sentences carefully and make them concise by
using all the preceding methods. Do not, however, sacrifice
concreteness and vividness for conciseness and brevity.

Excessively Concise
The garden has steps at both ends.

Concrete and Vivid
At each end of the sunken garden, worn granite steps, flanked by
large magnolia trees, lead to formal paths.

● *Exercise 7*

*Decide how to express the following sentences more con-
cisely.*

1. The custom which has always been so popular in the
   country of waving to strangers as you pass them is gradually fading out.

2. There are several reasons why officers of the law ought to be trained in the law of the land, and two of these are as follows. The first of these reasons is that policemen can enforce the law better if they are familiar with it. And second, they will be less likely to violate the rights of private citizens if they know exactly and accurately what these rights are.

3. Although the Kentucky rifle played an important and significant part in getting food for the frontier people of the American West, its function as a means of protection was in no degree any less significant in their lives.

4. Some television programs assume a low level of public intelligence and present their shows to the public as if the audience were made up of morons.

5. The distant explosion was audible to the ear.

6. The Japanese beetle is a beetle which was introduced into America from Japan and which thrives on fruits and roots of grass.

7. In modern warfare every nation which is engaged in the war broadcasts over radio and television information which is intended to convince the people in the enemy country that their cause is wrong.

8. It is not true that he is guilty.

9. It is a pleasure for some to indulge in eating large quantities of food at meals, but doctors of medicine tell us that such pleasures can only bring with them unpleasant results in the long run of things.

10. The essay consists of facts which vividly describe many of the events in the life of a typical juggler. In this description the author uses a vocabulary which is easy to understand. This vocabulary is on neither too high a level nor too low a level, but on one which can be understood by any high school graduate.

39 Repetition

Avoid careless repetition of words, phrases, sounds, and ideas. Repeat only for emphasis or clarity.

Unintentional repetition is seldom effective. Avoid repetition by (1) using synonyms, (2) using pronouns, and (3) condensing or combining sentences and omitting words.

Repetitious	Consideration for others is really the most important human quality. This quality comes from the heart.
Condensed	Consideration for others, which is really the most important human quality, comes from the heart.
Repetitious	Consideration for others is really the most important human quality. A person who has this trait is sincere.
Condensed	Sincere consideration for others is really the most important human quality.

39a Avoid repetition of sounds.

Devices like rhyme, meter, and repetition of sounds are a vital part of poetry, oratory, and some kinds of creative prose, but they are generally to be avoided in expository writing.

Rhyme	The biologist again *checked* the charts to determine the *effect* of the poison on the *insect*.
Correction	The biologist again studied the charts to determine the effect of the poison on the moth.
Repetition of Consonants	The *des*perate *dep*ression of that *d*ecade *d*oomed many people.
Correction	The severe depression of that time ruined many people.

39b Repeat a word or a phrase only for emphasis or for clarity.

Purposeful repetition of a word or a phrase often gains emphasis. Frequently repetition is used with maxims or sayings or in sentences that make statements about principles and abstractions.

Books and libraries preserve the *wisdom* of the ages, but not all *wisdom* comes from *books and libraries*.

Consistency may be regarded as a mark of *integrity*, but many a person of *integrity* does not define *consistency* as a great virtue.

• Exercise 8

Rewrite the following passage. Avoid wordiness and undesirable repetition.

A large number of people enjoy reading murder mysteries regularly. These people are not themselves murderers as a rule, nor would these people really ever enjoy seeing someone commit an actual murder, nor would most of them actually enjoy trying to solve an actual murder. They probably enjoy reading murder mysteries because of this reason: they have found a way to escape from the monotonous, boring routine of dull everyday existence.

To such people the murder mystery is realistic fantasy. It is realistic because the people in the murder mystery are as a general rule believable as people. They are not just made-up pasteboard figures. It is also realistic because the character who is the hero, the character who solves the murder mystery, solves it not usually by trial and error and haphazard methods but by exercising a high degree of logic and reason. It is absolutely and totally essential that people who enjoy murder mysteries have an admiration for the human faculty of logic.

But murder mysteries are also fantasies. The people who read such books of fiction play a game. It is a game in which they suspend certain human emotions. One of these human emotions that they suspend is pity. If readers stop to feel pity and sympathy for each and every victim that is killed or if readers stop to feel terrible horror that such a thing could happen in our world of today, they will never enjoy reading murder mysteries. The devoted reader of murder mysteries keeps uppermost in mind always and at all times the goal of arriving through logic and observation at the final solution to the mystery offered in the book. It is a game with life and death. Whodunits hopefully help the reader to hide from the hideous horrors of actual life and death in the real world.

40 Vagueness

Do not write vaguely. Choose words that are as specific
and as concrete as your meaning requires.

Avoid sentences which can have many different meanings.

> The weather was bad.

The preceding sentence could mean several things:

> Heavy rains caused a flash flood.
> The baseball game was rained out.
> During the drought all the crops failed except the peanuts.

Writing which is not specific can cause misunderstanding.
Abstract language draws general concepts from specific instances. The diagram below is a simple illustration; each step to
the right represents a further abstraction.

Concrete   **Increasingly Abstract**

Without the power to abstract, we would be bound to the immediate object or experience. We could never talk about "a
meal," but only "roast beef and a baked potato." Increasingly

abstract concepts like *meat, food, meal,* and *sustenance* allow us to group large numbers of objects, ideas, and experiences and to combine abstractions in order to discover still more relationships—in short, to think.

Abstractions like *food, drink,* and *sustenance* derive from concrete experience. High-level abstractions like *integrity, morality, freedom, goodness, love,* and *justice* are further removed from specific acts and objects. A high-level abstraction may cause difficulty because it means something a little different to almost everyone who uses the word. Because such abstractions as *democracy* and *liberty* are built on a complex of other abstractions, they are hard to define. Use them only with great care. Notice how the following passage improves as it becomes more specific and concrete.

General
Human beings need to recognize the geographical limitations of communities and the advantages of changes in environment. This principle is evident in the migrations of the creatures of nature.

More Specific
For the improvement of one's health, a change of environment is advisable. It is fortunate that no one place encompasses the world. The vegetation and birds of one place do not exist in another. Migratory birds are more cosmopolitan than people; they eat their meals each day in a different part of the country. Some other animals also follow the seasons.

Very Specific
To the sick the doctors wisely recommend a change of air and scenery. Thank Heaven, here is not all the world. The buckeye does not grow in New England, and the mockingbird is rarely heard here. The wild goose is more of a cosmopolite than we; he breaks his fast in Canada, takes a luncheon in the Ohio, and plumes himself for the night in a southern bayou. Even the bison, to some extent, keeps pace with the seasons, cropping the pastures of the Colorado only till a greener and sweeter grass awaits him by the Yellowstone. **HENRY DAVID THOREAU,** *Walden*

- *Exercise 9*

  Change words and details in the following sentences so that they become exact, concrete, specific.

  1. He consumed the food.
  2. She went across the street.
  3. The sunset was colorful.
  4. The vegetation was thick.
  5. The furniture was damaged.

- *Exercise 10*

  Write your personal definition of one of the following abstract terms in a paragraph of about two hundred words. Give concrete examples from your experience.

  courage   love   patriotism   humor

41 Connotation

Choose words with connotations appropriate to tone and content.

In addition to dictionary, or denotative, meanings, many words carry special associations or suggestions—**connotations.** The **denotation** of a word is its precise meaning, the exact definition given in a dictionary. Denotatively, a dog is a four-legged carnivorous domesticated mammal. Regarded in this way, the word *dog* arouses no emotional response of any kind, no hatred, no affection.

Connotations include emotional responses. What *dog* suggests to the reader or writer in addition to *four-legged carnivore* is connotation, which can be pleasant or unpleasant. To one person *dog* may suggest friendship; to another once attacked by a dog the word may connote terror.

A good writer uses connotations to evoke specific emotional reactions. The writer may evoke the rural, for example, by mentioning a *hound dog.* Consider the associations aroused by *cur, pooch, mutt, mongrel, puppy,* and *watchdog.* Even some breeds arouse different responses: *bloodhound, sheep dog, St. Bernard, poodle.*

Words that are close in meaning may have very different connotative overtones. Consider the following:

economical, thrifty, stingy
plump, fat, obese
slender, thin, skinny
resolute, strong-willed, stubborn

The exact writer avoids a word with unwanted connotations and chooses an appropriate substitute. Be sure that the words you choose give the suggestions you wish to convey. A single word with the wrong connotation can easily spoil a passage. Only one word has been changed in the following quotation:

Let us never bargain out of fear. But let us never fear to bargain.

President Kennedy actually wrote:

Let us never negotiate out of fear. But let us never fear to negotiate.

The word *bargain* ruins the tone of the statement even though it is fairly close in meaning to *negotiate.*

● *Exercise 11*

Words which have similar denotations frequently suggest responses that are quite different. The combinations below bring together words with different connotations. Rate each word for favorability of connotation:1 for most favorable, 2 for second, 3 for least. Be prepared to defend your decisions and to explain the different shades of connotation.

1. diseased
   ill
   sick
2. hate
   despise
   dislike
3. decay
   decompose
   rot
4. inexpensive
   cheap
   reasonable
5. enthusiast
   extremist
   fanatic
6. innocent
   naive
   simple
7. gaudy
   ornate
   showy
8. abnormal
   eccentric
   peculiar
9. odor
   stench
   smell
10. illegal
    criminal
    unethical

42 Figurative Language

Use fresh and imaginative figures of speech. Avoid mixed figures.

42a Use figurative comparisons.

Convey forceful impressions by comparing things that are not literally similar. Describe abstractions in concrete terms.

1. Write metaphors (implied comparisons).

   Historians constantly stir the ashes of the past.
   The mind is a house of many mirrors.

2. Write similes (comparisons stated with *like* or *as*).

   The records of history are *like* the remains of burned-out fires.
   The mind is *like* a house of many mirrors.

3. Use personification.

> the staring windows of the empty house
> the bearded oak

As you develop the habit of comparing things, good figures of speech may begin to come to you more easily.

42b Avoid mixed, worn-out, or inappropriate figures of speech.

Mixed	These corporations lashed out with legal loopholes.
Worn-Out	The promising young broker was ruined by the fickle finger of fate and the long arm of the law.
Inappropriate	Then, like a thief in the night, my father passed away.

43 Flowery Language

Avoid ornate or pretentious language.

Flowery language, sometimes called fine writing, is usually pompous and artificial. *These United States* rather than *the United States, in the year of 1978* rather than *in 1978, at this point in time* rather than *now*, for example, have the ring of affectation. *Green lawn*—or even *lawn*—is more natural than *verdant sward. Spade* or *shovel* is more natural than *simple instrument for delving into Mother Earth.* Sincerity disappears in the elaborate phrase that describes a teacher as a *toiler in the long and arduous labors of pedagogy.*

• *Exercise 12*

Revise the following sentences to eliminate flowery language.

1. The troupe of thespians presented a work by the immortal Bard of Avon.

2. Our glorious nation is going through a period of hideous peril.

3. The elderly gentleman at long last captured a finny denizen of the deep.

4. With herculean toil the budding young attorney prepared an oration.

5. The law officer of the fairer sex told the nefarious wrong-doer to cease and desist.

The Process
of Composition

44 Clear and Logical Thinking

Check any facts you use, and be certain of their accuracy.
Some thinking involves reasoning which cannot be based on
positive facts. For such interpretations, which cannot be proved
right or wrong, use common sense to avoid the erroneous and
the absurd.

44a Use only accurate and verified data.

Facts are demonstrable. They are the basis of judgments. A
writer should distinguish carefully between the facts and the
judgments derived from them and then explain how one
comes from the other.

Factual errors make the reader suspicious and lead to distrust
and doubt. The following statements are immediately suspect
because of errors of fact.

> Arthur Wegelin testified that he had entered the country on
> June 31, 1978. (The month of June has thirty days.)

> Only wealthy people buy original oil paintings. (The facts do
> not bear out this contention.)

44b Use reliable authorities.

Specialists in the same field may disagree. Therefore, in evaluating an authority you may use some of the following criteria and perhaps additional methods.

1. When was the work published? An old publication may contain superseded information.
2. Who published the work? University presses and well-established publishing houses employ well-informed consultants.
3. Have other authorities commented favorably on the work in reviews and elsewhere?
4. Is the presumed authority writing about his or her own field? (An atomic scientist may not be an expert on world records in baseball.)
5. Are the language and the tone reasonable, or does the authority attempt to persuade by using prejudiced and slanted words?
6. Is the authority fair-minded enough to admit the existence of facts that seem contradictory?
7. Does the authority distinguish fact from opinion, or are theories elevated to the level of indisputable fact?

44c Avoid sweeping generalizations.

Generalize with great care. If you know that three of your friends oppose capital punishment, you should not assert that "Everyone wishes to have capital punishment abolished" or even that "Most people wish to have capital punishment abolished." These statements are too broad for the evidence on which they are based. Sweeping generalizations like the following may contain some element of truth, but it is lost in the extremity of the statements.

A poor person cannot get a fair trial in the United States.

Soviet athletes are the best in the world.

44f

Sweeping generalizations about nationalities and races are among the most illogical and pernicious. If you have not done extensive and conclusive research on your subject, qualify your opinions.

> Some people feel that a poor person cannot get a fair trial in the United States.
>
> Some Soviet athletes are among the best in the world.

It will help you to resist the temptation to claim too much if you remember that a sweeping generalization is very often a falsification.

44d Use enough specific and accurate evidence to support your argument.

Truth and accuracy depend on an adequate number of examples. Statistics and samplings of opinions, polls, and other kinds of data should be not only sufficiently extensive but also fairly and representatively chosen. A public opinion poll taken from only one social, educational, or occupational group, for example, would probably be misleading.

44e Stick to the point.

Do not introduce irrelevancies or wander off the subject. First or last paragraphs of papers are sometimes especially irrelevant because they begin or end at a point too far removed from the subject. Digression is a sign of failure to focus attention on the problem at hand.

44f Do not ignore conflicting facts or evidence.

Be aware of facts and instances which seem to refute or qualify your views and conclusions. Deal with them fully and honestly.

You can actually strengthen your case by taking opposing evidence into consideration.

44g Do not beg the question or reason in a circle.

A writer who argues in a circle assumes that something is true and writes as if it had been proved.

Circular   A large part of the taxpayer's educational dollar is
Reasoning spent on unnecessary items like school lunchrooms, classes for handicapped children, and instruction in art and music.

That the educational items mentioned are "unnecessary" ones is a debatable proposition which the writer does not establish but merely asserts. The writer is begging the question (arguing in a circle) by simply restating the proposition.

44h Do not omit essential steps in thought or draw false conclusions from unstated assumptions.

A logical fallacy results whenever the omission of a step in reasoning leads to a false conclusion. The argument that "he cannot make the honor roll because he is a football player" is based on a false assumption: that no football player ever makes good grades. Similar omissions of parts of the argument occur in the following sentences. What are the unstated assumptions, and why are the conclusions false?

Since she made good grades in elementary school, she will undoubtedly be a good student in high school.

She will not make a good judge because she was once fined for speeding.

He has a wonderful personality and will certainly be a successful salesperson.

44i Do not substitute an appeal to emotions for an appeal to reason.

Name-calling is an appeal to prejudice. Calling an opponent a moron beclouds an issue. This is argument against a person rather than against a principle or a point of view.

Loaded words and **labels** attempt to shape an attitude through prejudice instead of reason. In loaded terms a government subsidy plan might become a "hand-out scheme that a bunch of radical do-gooders are trying to foist off on the taxpayers."

Flattery attempts to persuade through excessive praise. The political candidate who tells an audience that he knows they will vote for him because of their high intelligence is attempting to convince by flattering.

Snob appeal asserts that one should adopt a certain view because the better people do. The use of athletes, beauty queens, or motion picture stars in advertising testimonials is a form of snob appeal.

Mass appeal attempts to persuade by asserting that everyone follows a certain pattern. It suggests that one who does not follow the herd is in error (*everyone ought* to go to college; *everyone ought* to own a home). Mass appeal urges people to support a seemingly popular view—to climb on the bandwagon.

44j Do not draw false conclusions about cause and effect.

When two things happen in sequence, the second is not necessarily caused by the first. If a man walks under a ladder and shortly thereafter loses his wallet, he should not assume that he lost his wallet *because* he walked under the ladder. To show a cause-and-effect relationship between two events, it is necessary to produce evidence of real causation.

44k

44k Be moderate in tone.

Be temperate in your judgments and in your choice of words. Overstatement, overemphasis, and dogmatic assertion not only irritate most readers but arouse doubt or even disbelief. The good writer knows better than to be cocksure and brash.

44L Allow for adequate alternatives.

On some questions it is false logic to assume that there are *two and only two* alternatives. Often other possibilities exist. If, for example, a mother tells her son that he must go to college or fail in life, she has not recognized that her son may succeed without a college education.

• *Exercise 1*

Describe the errors in content and thought in each of the following.

1. The fact that the dictionary expert wrote the publisher about his objections to the novel proves that as fiction it was not worth publishing.

2. Boys are good in mathematics and science; girls are good in English and the fine arts.

3. Soviet medicine is far behind medicine in this country because the Soviet Union has so many young doctors.

4. Anyone who reaches the age of eighteen is old enough to make decisions without advice from other people.

5. John Quincy Adams, the second President of the United States, was respected for his idealism and great knowledge.

6. Nearly all the great monuments of this world are made of marble.

7. All college graduates are unusually intelligent; otherwise, they could not have passed the courses and completed their education.

8. The fact that you could espouse the cause of those rebels shows me that you are a dangerous radical.

9. After only one week at Reduso Spa, Mrs. Wentworth lost sixteen pounds. Enroll now if you really wish to lose weight.

10. All young people should go to trade school instead of college because it is extremely difficult for people to get good jobs unless they can do something with their hands.

11. Order our new device for restoring hair in your bald spots, and new hair will begin to grow within two weeks.

12. Her parents deserted her when she was an infant. No wonder she has spent much of her life in prison.

13. The welfare system in this country makes the people who have earned their money give it away to lazy good-for-nothings who are not willing to work for themselves.

14. Joseph Conrad was the greatest novelist who ever lived.

15. The Establishment has arrived at dependable rules of conduct; those who follow them will have no serious problems.

16. Freedom is a necessary ingredient in the life of every woman, and every woman should make her decisions without advice because of her need for liberation.

17. Subscribe to *Now,* the intellectual's magazine, and join the most enlightened readers of the day.

18. Shakespeare did not write the plays attributed to him. This fact has been proved by a famous surgeon who recently retired from a medical career to which he had devoted almost all his energy.

19. Who says fortunetellers are fakes? Just as the palmist said, I went to Alaska three months after she told my fortune.

20. A good paper must be written in chronological order.

45 Writing Good Paragraphs

A **paragraph** usually develops one central purpose or idea. For the writer careful paragraphing is an aspect of accurate thinking and logical organization. For the reader clear and orderly paragraphs help comprehension by marking thought units and giving a sense of separation and progression. If sentences are the boards and bricks of the house of writing, and the paper is the entire structure, paragraphs are the rooms. Some papers are written with such long paragraphs that they are like houses with few rooms. Other papers are so frequently divided that they are like houses with rooms no larger than closets.

45a Express the main idea of a paragraph in a topic sentence.

Most paragraphs contribute one block of thought within the paper, and usually that thought is summed up in one predominant sentence. The connection of that **topic sentence** to others like it in surrounding paragraphs should be easily apparent, and it should also be clear how the other sentences in the paragraph are tied to the dominant sentence and how they are related to each other. Nearly always the topic sentence comes at the beginning of a paragraph because that is where the reader needs to know the direction of the paragraph. A topic sentence supplies that direction. The other sentences develop the main idea by giving reasons or examples or adding details, but as a rule they do not control the purpose of the paragraph or primarily reveal where the paper is going. Consequently, taken together, the topic sentences should show a writer whether the lines of thought are clear in the paper. Usually the topic sentences will also enable a reader to scan a piece of writing and to see generally what its major points are.

Test your own papers by topic sentences. If they move logically and clearly through the main outlines of your work, that is a good sign. If not, you may have omitted ideas, arranged thoughts in the wrong sequence, or neglected to state purpose and direction. Then you may need to replan your paper, to discard or move paragraphs, to add new ones, and to rewrite topic sentences. When the basic structure seems effective, then you may begin to look more intently within the paragraph.

The following selection from an article on George Washington illustrates a skillful author's methods of writing good topic sentences and presenting the details that support them. The topic sentences are italicized.

At the simplest, most superficial level Washington's love of honor showed itself in a concern with outward appearances. His attachment to Mount Vernon, for example, did not stop at the desire to make a profit from it. He wanted the place and its surroundings to look right, to honor the owner by the way they looked; and this meant giving up the slovenly, though often profitable, agricultural practices of his neighbors. He stopped growing tobacco and turned to the rotation of cereal crops that were approved by the English agricultural reformers of the time. He tried, mostly in vain, to substitute handsome English hedgerows for the crude rail fences of Virginia. And he insisted that all weeds and brush be grubbed out of his plowed fields, not simply for the sake of productivity, but because the fields looked better that way. He would rather, he said, have one acre properly cleansed than five prepared in the usual way.

Similarly, as commander-in-chief, he wanted his soldiers to look well. Their uniforms must be kept in order and "well put on." Otherwise, he said, there would be "little difference in *appearance* between a soldier in rags and a soldier in uniform." Appearance mattered especially to him when French troops were coming: his army must not be dishonored by looking shabby or careless. Even the huts for winter quarters must be built of an identical size: "any hut not exactly conformable to the plan, or the least out of line, shall be pulled down and built again agreeable to the model and in its proper place." And when Washington became president, he showed the same concern for appearances in furnishing his house and decorating his coach in a plain but elegant style that he thought was appropriate for the head of a republican government.

But a man who craved honor could not gain it simply by putting up a good appearance. This was only a shade removed from vanity, and Washington from the beginning betrayed none of the vanity of a John Adams. Indeed, his concern with appearances included a horror of appearing vain. He would not assist would-be biographers for fear, he confessed to a friend, of having "vanity or ostentation imputed to me." He would not even allow Arthur Young, the great English agricultural reformer with whom he corresponded, to publish extracts from the letters, for fear of seeming ostentatious or of giving occasion for some "officious tongue to use my name with indelicacy."

EDMUND S. MORGAN, *"George Washington:
The Aloof American"*

The paragraphs are related, and the italicized topic sentences indicate that the passage is about Washington's concern for order and for what the author calls "outward appearances." The first two paragraphs are arranged by Washington's concern for appearances in his different occupations—his farming and his serving as a military officer. The last sentence of the second paragraph shows how he carried the same quality on to higher office. The third paragraph is more general; it shows how the characteristic discussed in all the paragraphs is a trait of the whole man, and it introduces a final and crucial point—that Washington was not really vain but rather was concerned that others might think he was. The three paragraphs are unified and coherent because each topic sentence introduces a unit of thought that contributes to an overall picture of the man.

45b Write unified paragraphs. Be sure that each sentence is clearly related to the main idea.

Every sentence in a good paragraph bears on the main point. An irrelevant sentence first subtracts from the main point and then gives the reader difficulty in getting back to the subject. A good paragraph does not change its course and remain there or switch off to another point and then attempt to return. Notice how in the following paragraph the writer digresses less than halfway through and destroys unity:

> Groups of people often have something like a definable and single personality, and one group may differ markedly from another of a similar kind. For example, baseball teams in the same league are often widely different in personality. As a group a team may be lazy or energetic, amenable or quarrelsome, bright or dull, and so on. The manager of one team may find his job enjoyable, and the manager of another may drag his feet with disappointment. Of course, managers differ as much as their teams do. One may be generous with his time and truly concerned about his players. Another may be selfish and indifferent. I have known managers who disliked even talking with their own players. Different as groups like baseball teams are, it is almost impossible to define what causes the great divergences from one to another.

The writer of this paragraph set out to discuss the idea that groups of people seem to have a personality much as individuals do. Had the idea been sustained, it would have made an excellent paragraph. It does not succeed because the writer got off the track and addressed the subject of baseball managers. The temptation to digress is often great when the mind runs ahead to other interesting thoughts. Consequently, mental discipline is one of the most important requirements for writing good paragraphs. The final sentence of the paragraph turns to yet another subject—causes—and should probably be the first sentence of a new paragraph instead of the last sentence of this one.

• *Exercise 2*

Three of the following paragraphs are not unified; as many as three sentences in a paragraph may be extraneous. Decide which paragraphs need revision, and determine which sentences in them ought to be deleted. Identify the topic sentence of each paragraph.

PARAGRAPH 1

A Saturday visit to the barber shop was once an exciting and meaningful experience for a boy. It offered an almost unique opportunity for a youngster to enter the adult masculine world for a little while. At school a boy had no opportunity to see this world. At home he was often with his father and perhaps his brothers, but that was not the same as sitting among men and listening to their jokes and their strong opinions on people and politics and their stories, sometimes of violence and courage. If he was wise, the lad sat in the barber chair and listened carefully with silent respect, for he sensed that he was being given the rare opportunity of visiting a world he would someday enter.

PARAGRAPH 2

As the basic social unit the family is as important today in America as it ever was, though perhaps in a different way. Family coherence was essential in the early days of the country to insure the survival of the individual members. They helped each other and protected each other. Today people need their families not so much to insure physical survival as to help them through the perils of modern times, especially through such psychological perils as loss of identity. America is not all bad, however. It offers the greatest freedom of all countries for individual development. America is still the land of opportunity. The family gives one a sense of belonging, a sense of the past. When all else seems severed, the family can be the anchor to sanity.

PARAGRAPH 3

Sensible people who deal in realities every day will often go out of their way on the street to avoid walking under a ladder. When they spill salt, diners in restaurants throw a little over their shoulders to ward off bad luck. It is not at all unusual to see a perfectly sane adult knock on wood to insure continued good fortune. Many people moan over broken mirrors not because the accident will cost them the money to buy new mirrors but because they are worried that they may be in for seven years of bad luck. Superstitions, then, are many and various and still manifest themselves in the actions of a great many normal people.

PARAGRAPH 4

Pollution is a more complex issue than it may appear to be on the surface. Consumers wish to have clean air, but they hesitate to pay more for the mechanism on cars that will help insure it. They want clean water, but they sometimes complain of the costs that are passed on to them of new sewage-disposal plants. Yet the public is correct in its desire for more ecological controls, and at the same time its unwillingness to spend an increasingly large amount of money for them is understandable. Overpopulation is another threat to the future. The world population is growing at an alarming rate. If this fact is not recognized and if steps are not taken now to slow down population growth, our children's children may experience a frightening drop in the quality of life on earth. City dwellers would like to diminish noise pollution, but they are naturally hesitant to take steps that would eliminate such noise polluters as automobiles from their downtown streets. Pollution is thus not a simple problem to be overcome by a single act of legislation.

PARAGRAPH 5

The theme of the motion picture *All Quiet on the Western Front* is one of anti-war protest. The film deals with World War I from a German perspective. The hero has a professor he first admires but comes to distrust. Even though it is about Germans, the picture does not glorify the German cause. It depicts the plight of the sensitive human spirit caught in the terrible grip of war. World War I started when Archduke Ferdinand was assassinated. Probably no one would have guessed that this incident would grow quickly into the greatest war the world had ever known. At the end of the film the hero is killed while reaching for a flower he sees on the battlefield.

45c Avoid short, skimpy paragraphs.

Short paragraphs are sometimes standard and effective in news items, fiction, dialogue, and descriptions of dramatic action. The length of a paragraph is usually decided by the importance and complexity of its central idea, the richness of detail that develops it, and even the number of words allowed in an assignment. Paragraphs in a paper of 600 words will generally be shorter and more uniform in length than those in a paper of 1500 to 2000 words. Thought should never be divided into paragraphs simply at mechanical intervals.

In most expository prose a series of short, choppy paragraphs suggests undeveloped ideas or simply the writer's failure to put paragraph divisions at good places. Sometimes several short paragraphs can be combined under the one which has the strongest topic sentence, perhaps the only possible topic sentence in the group. The following passage, from the beginning of an article, is chopped up excessively, and its divisions are not always logical.

> Streams of electrons and protons crash continuously into our atmosphere, stripping electrons off the nitrogen molecules and oxygen atoms and providing energy for the spectacular sky show we in the Northern Hemisphere know as the aurora borealis, or northern lights.
> This phenomenon has intrigued philosophers since an-

cient times. Today scientists are trying to find out what happens when up to a trillion watts of power are injected into the upper atmosphere, producing heat, x rays, ionized particles, and, when viewed from space, more light than all the cities of North America.

The basic forces at work are still not clear, and we don't know what effects all this energy has on weather, climate, the ozone layer, and biological processes.

But knowledge is increasing by the year. Descriptions of the aurora appear in the mythology of the Eskimos and the Scandinavians. Northern Germanic tribes considered auroras to be the shields of the Valkyrie warrior-women.

The Australian Aborigines thought the aurora australis (southern lights) to be the gods' campfires; and the natives of Ceylon revered it as a message from Buddha. Mentions of the aurora borealis are not uncommon in Greek and Roman writings; major displays were recorded and analyzed by Aristotle, Pliny the Elder, Seneca, and others.

THOMAS A. POTEMRA, "Aurora borealis:
the greatest light show on earth"

Actually, the passage was written as three paragraphs, the second beginning, "Descriptions of the aurora . . ." and the third beginning, "Mentions of the aurora. . . ." Notice that the first paragraph introduces the subject of scientists' interest in the aurora borealis and the next two, shorter, paragraphs deal with (1) the aurora in mythology and (2) the aurora in ancient writings. When the passage is divided properly into three paragraphs, continuity is improved and the logic of the thought becomes clearer.

Streams of electrons and protons crash continuously into our atmosphere, stripping electrons off the nitrogen molecules and oxygen atoms and providing energy for the spectacular sky show we in the Northern Hemisphere know as the aurora borealis, or northern lights. This phenomenon has intrigued philosophers since ancient times. Today scientists are trying to find out what happens when up to a trillion watts of power are injected into the upper atmosphere, producing heat, x rays, ionized particles, and, when viewed from space, more light than all the cities of North America. The basic forces at work are still not clear, and we don't know what effects all this energy has on weather, climate, the ozone layer, and biological processes. But knowledge is increasing by the year.

Descriptions of the aurora appear in the mythology of the Eskimos and the Scandinavians. Northern Germanic tribes considered auroras to be the shields of the Valkyrie warrior-women. The Australian Aborigines thought the aurora australis (southern lights) to be the gods' campfires; and the natives of Ceylon revered it as a message from Buddha.

Mentions of the aurora borealis are not uncommon in Greek and Roman writings; major displays were recorded and analyzed by Aristotle, Pliny the Elder, Seneca, and others.

45d Avoid excessively long paragraphs.

Very long paragraphs make it hard for a reader to digest meaning easily. To reduce excessive length, it may be necessary to reduce the scope of the controlling idea. But sometimes a paragraph can be trimmed simply by discarding material. You may not need ten examples to prove or illustrate a point. Four or five may do it just as well.

• *Exercise 3*

Decide how to make two paragraphs out of the following passage. (Sentences are in their original order.)

Both radio and phonograph fostered the continued popularity of dancing, which had swept the twenties under the heady inspiration of jazz, that powerful if almost indefinable rhythmic style.

About 1931, when a popular song was urging the depressed to "wrap your troubles in dreams, and dream your troubles away," the plangent bravado of jazz temporarily faded from fashion before the soothing hypnotic strains of "sweet" bands like those of Guy Lombardo, Wayne King, and Eddy Duchin.

An advance-guardist of new modes in jazz who died in that year—the trumpeter Leon ("Bix") Beiderbecke—would later be recalled nostalgically by Dorothy Baker's fine novel of the artist as jazzman, *Young Man with a Horn* (1938).

Early in 1934, perhaps as a harbinger of recovery, the spirit of jazz was reborn, largely by the superb clarinet recordings and dance-band broadcasts of Benny Goodman, exponent of what European connoisseurs called *le jazz hot*.

It soon gained a new name, swing. A more dynamic form of syncopation and superimposed rhythm, an intense yet easy floating that "gets there on time"—and in expert hands capable of rich improvisation—swing retained the essence of its parent, jazz.

" 'Swing' is to jazz what the poetic spirit is to poetry," wrote one lyric journalist in the winter of 1935–1936, when "jam sessions" and Hot Clubs were springing up over the nation.

An incidental term in high favor was "boogie-woogie," signifying piano music in which an insistent rolling left-hand pattern mingled with the fancy-free inventions of the right.

DIXON WECTER, *The Age of the Great Depression, 1929–1941*

● *Exercise 4*

The following passages were originally divided into three and four paragraphs. Determine where you believe the authors made the divisions, and identify the topic sentences.

As early as the 1830's, growing urbanization in the Northeast had made a substantial impression upon the nature of agriculture in that region. In the immediate vicinity of burgeoning factory towns and commercial centers, farmers were concentrating their energy upon supplying local markets with fresh vegetables, fruits, and dairy products. In outlying districts farmers had begun to specialize in the raising of beef or pork, or in the production of wool for the region's new textile industry. Farmers who participated in this commercial economy soon abandoned the old practice of home manufacture which, in the past, had been an inseparable part of farm life. Store-bought cloth replaced homespun, and factory-made furniture and farm tools were substituted for homemade ones. By 1840 the expanding urban centers of the Northeast were being supplied not only with produce from Eastern farms, but also with produce from farther west. A steady stream of Western wheat, beef, pork, wool, and cheese was flowing into Eastern markets. Some of this produce had been moved down the Mississippi River by steamer, then shipped up the Eastern Seaboard to Philadelphia, New York, Boston, and other ports. A larger portion had come by way of the Great Lakes and the Erie Canal. In the following decade the flow of Western goods would continually swell as a network of railroad lines spread through the new states, connecting areas previously cut off from markets. In 1850 there were only 9,000 miles of railroad track in the country; no more than ten years later there were 30,000 miles. By the middle of the century Western farmers were finding a steady market for their goods in Europe as well as at home. Rapid industrialization in Britain and on the continent had created huge urban populations and an increasing demand for cheap foodstuffs. In 1850 the United States exported 11 million bushels of wheat and 3 million bushels of corn. During the next decades exports would climb to higher and higher levels. By 1897 wheat exports had risen to 217 million bushels and corn to 212 million. In peak years one third of the United States wheat crop was shipped abroad. Meat exports, which had been relatively insignificant before the Civil War, amounted to $179 million a year by the end of the century. Like the cotton farmer of the South, the Northern grain or livestock farmer had become vitally dependent upon foreign markets.

MAISIE AND RICHARD CONRAT, *"How U.S. farmers became specialists—in cash and debts"*

The Sargasso Sea is a place forgotten by the winds, undisturbed by the strong flow of waters that girdle it as with a river. Under the seldom-clouded skies, its waters are warm and heavy with salt. Separated widely from coastal rivers and from polar ice, there is no inflow of fresh water to dilute its saltiness; the only influx is of saline water from the adjacent currents, especially from the Gulf Stream or North Atlantic Current as it crosses from America to Europe. And with the little, inflowing streams of surface water come the plants and animals that for months or years have drifted in the Gulf Stream. The sargassum weeds are brown algae belonging to several species. Quantities of the weeds live attached to reefs or rocky outcroppings off the coasts of the West Indies and Florida. Many of the plants are torn away by storms, especially during the hurricane season. They are picked up by the Gulf Stream and are drifted northward. With the weeds go, as involuntary passengers, many small fishes, crabs, shrimps, and innumerable larvae of assorted species of marine creatures, whose home had been the coastal banks of sargassum weed. Curious things happen to the animals that have ridden on the sargassum weed into a new home. Once they lived near the sea's edge, a few feet or a few fathoms below the surface, but never far above a firm bottom. They knew the rhythmic movements of waves and tides. They could leave the shelter of the weeds at will and creep or swim about over the bottom in search of food. Now, in the middle of the ocean, they are in a new world. The bottom lies two or three miles below them. Those who are poor swimmers must cling to the weed, which now represents a life raft, supporting them above the abyss. Over the ages since their ancestors came here, some species have developed special organs of attachment, either for themselves or for their eggs, so that they may not sink into the cold, dark water far below. The flying fish make nests of the weed to contain their eggs, which bear an amazing resemblance to the sargassum floats or "berries." Indeed, many of the little marine beasts of the weedy jungle seem to be playing an elaborate game of disguise in which each is camouflaged to hide it from the others. The Sargasso sea slug—a snail without a shell—has a soft, shapeless brown body spotted with dark-edged circles and fringed with flaps and folds of skin, so that as it creeps over the weed in search of prey it can scarcely be distinguished from the vegetation. One of the fiercest carnivores of the place, the sargassum fish Pterophryne, has copied with utmost fidelity the branching fronds of the weed, its golden berries, its rich brown color, and even the white dots of encrusting worm tubes. All these elaborate bits of mimicry are indications of the fierce internecine wars of the Sargasso jungles, which go on without quarter and without mercy for the weak or the unwary.

RACHEL CARSON, *The Sea Around Us*

45e Develop your paragraphs adequately.

Do not omit the examples, the proof, the explanations, the exceptions—in short, the finer and the fuller details that make good paragraphs. Instead of merely mentioning points, you should develop and clarify them for the reader. Details flesh out your ideas.

The following three topic sentences alone lack the fullness of good writing. The basic principles are introduced, but nothing is developed:

Most of American history and much of American literature have been conditioned or influenced by the existence of a changing frontier.

Until recently, a politician who had not been born in a log cabin was handicapped in any election.

For Americans the frontier has always been an ambivalent symbol.

In the paragraphs as they were originally written, the subject—the frontier—comes alive:

> Most of American history and much of American literature have been conditioned or influenced by the existence of a changing frontier. In our homes and in our schools many of our greatest stories and legends are about men like Captain John Smith, Lewis and Clark, Daniel Boone, Davy Crockett, and Kit Carson. We celebrate not only Washington's achievements as our Revolutionary leader and first President, but also his exploits as . . . [a] surveyor of the wilderness. We remember Andrew Jackson as Old Hickory, a frontier figure. We honor Abraham Lincoln as a son of the prairie woodland, a rail-splitter who read the Bible by light from a fireplace.
>
> Until recently, a politician who had not been born in a log cabin was handicapped in any election. Theodore Roosevelt gained glamor from his career as a cattleman and his fame as the organizer of the Rough Riders. Even a New Englander like Calvin Coolidge found it wise to visit the Black Hills of South Dakota and wear an Indian headdress for newspaper photographers. And in 1960 we elected as President another New Englander, who promised us a "New Frontier."
>
> For Americans the frontier has always been an ambivalent symbol. It has been considered a source of freedom and a place of danger; an exciting challenge, but also a cause of hardship and exhaustion; a place for heroism, but also an excuse for racism, sadism, and brutality; an inexhaustible mine of humor, but humor too often tinged with cruelty or false sentimentality. It has been idealized as a source of health, vitality, and nobility; but it has been condemned as rude, ugly, and barbaric.
>
> PHILLIP DURHAM AND EVERETT L. JONES,
> *The Frontier in American Literature*

In the first two paragraphs the topic sentences are developed by references to typical and famous Americans related in some way to the frontier. In the last paragraph interpretation is more significant, and the qualities of the frontier and its people are the basis of development.

45f Develop a paragraph by the method most appropriate for the central topic.

Paragraphs may develop their topics in many ways. They may define, classify, or move from cause to effect or effect to cause, from a generalization to the facts it interprets, from a body of facts to a generalization about them. Usually the material on a subject so clearly dictates its pattern that the writer does not even have to decide to write a paragraph of a certain kind— definition, for example. The writer simply defines without deciding to do so, because defining is what the material demands. If the subject and material are considered, the method takes care of itself. There are, however, a few points to keep in mind.

Climactic order   Almost any list is more interesting if you begin with the least important item and end with the most important.

Comparison and contrast   Two basic methods can be used in developing a paragraph by comparison and contrast: writing everything about one point and then everything about the other (XXXX YYYY); or writing about alternating points throughout the paragraph (XY XY XY XY). Either method can be effective, but in long and complex comparisons and contrasts the alternating method is generally better.

Definition   Good expository definition tries to explain an abstraction clearly and accurately. The problem is to make the term sufficiently concrete in examples which do not excessively restrict the meaning. Intellectual definitions, of course, may be much more elaborate than the definitions given in dictionaries.

45g Use transitions to show relationships between sentences within paragraphs and between one paragraph and another.

Transitional devices help your reader see how you progress from one point to another and how your ideas are related.

Connective Words and Expressions

but	indeed	likewise
and	in fact	consequently
however	meanwhile	first
moreover	afterward	next
furthermore	then	in brief
on the other hand	so	to summarize
nevertheless	still	to conclude
for example	after all	similarly

Demonstratives (References to demonstratives must be clear.)

this   that   these   those

Other Pronouns

many   each   some   others   all   either

Repeated key words, phrases, and synonyms are good signposts to guide the reader from sentence to sentence and paragraph to paragraph.

Transitional words in topic sentences can contribute to clarity, coherence, and the movement of the discussion. Some writers guide readers with a connector at the beginning of almost every paragraph. H. J. Muller, for example, begins a sequence of paragraphs about science as follows:

> In this summary, science . . .
> Yet science does . . .
> Similarly the basic interests of science . . .
> In other words, they are not . . .
> This demonstration that even the scientist . . .
> This idea will concern us . . .
> In other words, facts and figures . . .

45g

● *Exercise 5*

From the three possible topic sentences for each of the following paragraphs, choose the most appropriate. As you read the paragraphs, notice not only the topic sentences but also the use of detail, unity, order or sequence, and transitions. The paragraphs were taken from Dixon Wecter's The Age of the Great Depression, 1929–1941.

PARAGRAPH 1
A. Several things happened in the late 1930's.
B. The success of radio can be traced to several factors.
C. Fashions in radio entertainment came and went.

   After the success in 1936 of "Professor Quiz," question-and-answer programs like "Information Please" and "The Quiz Kids" burgeoned mightily. Such unrehearsed contests reflected a vogue similar to that featuring sidewalk interviews, guessing games, and amateur hours, with a large element of audience participation. The radio serial proved to be a universal favorite, illustrated early in the era by the vast popularity of "Amos 'n' Andy" . . . or the plenitude of "soap operas" which later in the decade came to rule the daytime hours, dedicated to the praise of soap flakes and washing powders between interstices of tears and laughter in their plots of homely romance. For juveniles the decade's hero was the "Lone Ranger," who made his debut in 1933—a stalwart without fear or vices, whose cry "Hi-yo, Silver!" heralded his arrival upon that trusty steed to redress wrong and succor the weak. By the close of the era radio's best-known personality had come to be an impudent puppet named Charlie McCarthy, creation of the ventriloquist Edgar Bergen.

PARAGRAPH 2
A. Music was immensely popular in the 1930's, although not as popular as it would become in the 1940's.
B. Music occupied over half of radio's daily log, and more of it than ever before was of high quality.

C. Radio was immensely popular in the 1930's—more so than it ever would be again.

In 1930 Columbia began its Sunday broadcasting of New York Philharmonic concerts; the following year the National Broadcasting Company launched its Saturday-afternoon series of grand operas from the Metropolitan; in 1937 it persuaded the world-famous conductor Arturo Toscanini to undertake a memorable series with its own symphony orchestra. Over ten million families, according to a 1939 estimate, listened to such music; a poll in this year indicated that, save on the farm and at the bottom of the economic scale, those who enjoyed "classical" music outnumbered those desiring exclusively "popular." When in 1940 the Metropolitan Opera Company in severe financial straits appealed to its invisible audience, they contributed a third of a million dollars to "save the Met."

PARAGRAPH 3

A. Music appreciation in the home saw the performer's role steadily supplanted, however, by the auditor's.
B. Musical appreciation was of a very high order.
C. Radio programs encouraged listeners to perform music in their homes.

While the radio was outstripping even the phonograph in popularity, father's fiddle gathered dust, and in affluent homes the piano remained oftentimes as a piece of prestige furniture. In 1939 only sixteen million copies of sheet music were sold as compared with forty-five million records of popular melodies. The invasion of music by radio, whether "live" or "canned," was greater still, though harder to measure, while the life expectancy of a popular song, under furious exploitation by the "Lucky Strike Hit Parade" and similar programs, grew vastly shorter.

• Exercise 6

The sentences in the following paragraphs were taken from Dixon Wecter's The Age of the Great Depression, 1929–

1941. *The sentences are not in their original order within paragraphs. Determine the proper sequence within each group.*

PARAGRAPH 1

A. Recordings of these speeches through the years show changes in Roosevelt's technique, from the old-fashioned sonorous style with oratorical pauses learned in preradio days, to a lower pitch and softer, relaxed, more engaging address better suited to the unseen audience.

B. The New Deal's best radio propagandist was President Roosevelt himself, whose warm democratic salutation "My friends" had been adopted as early as his vain campaign for the vice-presidency in 1920.

C. His direct, intimate appeal to the people built a personal leadership unprecedented in its influence; not infrequently fifty thousand letters a day followed a "fireside chat."

PARAGRAPH 2

A. Based upon H. G. Wells's *War of the Worlds* and punctuated by announcements that should have carried reassurance, the sketch purported to describe a rocket-borne invasion of Martians, equipped with flame throwers and heat rays, who proceeded to ravage the New Jersey countryside until slain by the disease bacteria of this planet.

B. Not only did it [radio] carry nuances and subtle emotion denied to print, but it tended to arrest in the listener those critical impulses that often led a reader to turn back to the dubious or imperfectly understood.

C. Not pausing for that dénouement, at least a million auditors became upset or terror-stricken, many forsaking their homes afoot or by car in panic.

D. Startling evidence of its hypnotic effect on the mass imagination was afforded by a broadcast of the young actor Orson Welles on the evening of October 30, 1938, a month after the Munich crisis.

PARAGRAPH 3

A. While newspaper advertising never regained its 1929 peak of eight hundred million dollars, radio salesmanship mounted year by year until in 1941 it was doing a two-hundred-million-dollar business—over a third of that vouchsafed its competitor—with magazines occupying third place.

B. The potency of the air waves was not overlooked by the advertiser.

C. Growing constantly more blatant, radio advertising featured the singing commercial, the middle commercial flanked by those incidental opening and closing plugs called by the trade "cowcatchers" and "hitchhikers," and the "give-away" to reward a listener's correct answer to a telephone call from the studio.

PARAGRAPH 4

A. Within the single year 1935 the number of stations so owned doubled, and by 1940 no less than a third of the nation's eight hundred licensed stations were tied in one way or another to newspapers. . . .

B. At the same time newspapers rapidly increased their ownership of radio stations, sometimes monopolizing all the news outlets in a given community.

C. Helpless to throttle the radio as an advertising medium, the newspaper press for a time tried to prevent its access to a regular flow of the world's news.

D. In 1934, however, the feud was composed by the so-called press-radio agreement and formation of the Transradio Press Service, which outlasted that pact.

46 Writing Good Papers

Stages in the process of composition overlap, but they can be separated for discussion. These include choosing and limiting a subject; determining your purpose and planning the development of your paper, often through an outline; writing the first draft; and revising and preparing the final draft. Allow yourself enough time so that you can think about your subject and plan adequately.

46a Choose a subject that interests you.

To find significant and interesting subjects, draw on your experience, memory, imagination, knowledge, interests, and studies. Good subjects can come to mind at unexpected moments. You may think of one while your thoughts are wandering in class or while you are going home on the bus. Never let a possible subject escape you. Reserve a page or two in your notebook for all the topics and titles which occur to you. Even the less promising possibilities may evolve into good subjects. When a paper must be written, it is better to have an excess of ideas than a blank sheet of paper staring at you from your desk. You can avoid false starts and lost time by examing your list of possibilities and settling on one good topic at the outset. (For suggestions about subjects for papers see pages 199–202.)

46b Limit your topic.

Tailor your subject to the length of the assignment. Do not skim the surface of a broad topic, but select a limited part of it and develop that part fully through discussion, analysis, illustration, and detail.

A 250-word paper calls for a more limited treatment than a 500-word or a 1000-word paper; it may demand a different subject altogether. Generalized treatments of large subjects can be successful if they are handled with intelligence, breadth of perspective, and insight; many good editorials are written on just such topics. But the best papers usually are limited enough to allow room for plenty of explanation and detail.

Suppose a student starts with the idea of writing a 500-word paper on humor. The evolution of this subject in the student's mind can be shown as follows:

Humor: Too broad . . .

The Nature of Humor: Still too broad . . .

A Specific Kind of Humor: Might have something here . . . think of a kind . . .

Sick Humor: Sounds unpleasant . . . unattractive topic equals unattractive paper?

Jokes and Jokers: Getting close, but still too broad . . .

Practical Jokers: Almost have it, but what about practical jokers?

The Serious Intent of Practical Jokers: That's it. A subject I'm interested in and can say something about.

Through association of ideas, this student has arrived at what looks like a workable subject.

Even after the topic is thus limited, however, you cannot *know* that it is the right size until you have (1) considered its subdivisions and (2) sometimes actually written the paper. A subject which at first seems limited may open up into greater complexity and promise to yield a paper far beyond the assigned length. If so, you must turn to another subject—perhaps a still more limited aspect of the first.

Or if the paper is already written, you may reduce the length of it, usually by cutting out whole sections. But a paper shortened in this way is often confused, jerky, or badly proportioned because of omissions and condensations. A fresh start with a new topic may cost a high price in lost time. It is much better to write a paper of the proper length in the first place.

46c Formulate a thesis statement.

The central idea of a paper can usually be expressed in a single sentence. Sometimes this statement can be phrased early in the planning process, sometimes not until you are near the actual writing. In any event, it should be expressed early in the written paper, often in the opening paragraph.

A good **thesis statement** is specific and concise. It brings the subject into focus for the reader, suggests the scope of the paper, and shows coherently the idea or ideas that the paper will develop.

Vague and Stereotyped	It is the purpose of this essay to discuss the serious intent of practical jokers.
Vague	Practical jokers have similar motivations.
More Purposeful	Practical jokers have four basic motivations: to obtain applause, to feel reassurance, to experience power, and to vent hostility.

46d Select an appropriate tone and be consistent.

Tone is the quality which reveals the writer's attitude toward the subject matter. The tone of a piece of writing may be serious or humorous, ironical or straightforward, zealous or casual, brisk or nostalgic. As a general rule, a moderately serious tone is the most effective for most subjects. Unless you are extremely skilled, you should not run the risk of alienating your reader by treating a serious subject humorously. Whatever tone you choose, be consistent. An inconsistent tone confuses a reader about the writer's intention. On the other hand, the tone need not be held unvaryingly in one key. It may, for example, move reasonably from the serious to a touch of humor, but it should not run from one extreme to another in the same piece of writing.

NOTE   Avoid flippancy and sarcasm.

46e Organize carefully.

You should never set out to write a paper without some kind of outline, even if it is only in your mind. A **scratch outline** is the simplest kind. It is a list of the points you want to make, in any form you wish. It is a quick way to order your thoughts and remind you of that order when you are writing the paper. For brief papers or those written during the class hour, a scratch outline will usually suffice. The following is a scratch outline for a paper on "The Serious Intent of Practical Jokers":

> practical jokes—variety of
> serious motivations
> to get attention
> to be reassured
> to experience power
> to vent hostility

A **topic outline** is a formal and detailed structure to help you organize your materials. In making a topic outline, observe these rules:

1. Number the main topics with roman numerals, the subtopics with capital letters, the details with Arabic numerals. If further subheadings are necessary, use a, b, c, and (1), (2), (3).

```
 I. ...........................................................
    A. .......................................................
       1. ...................................................
          a. ................................................
             (1) ...........................................
             (2) ...........................................
          b. ................................................
       2. ...................................................
    B. .......................................................
II. ...........................................................
```

2. Use parallel grammatical structures.

3. Use topics, not sentences. Do not place periods after the topics.

4. Check to see that your outline covers the subject completely.

5. Use specific topics and subheadings arranged in a logical, meaningful order. Each indented level of the outline represents a division of the preceding level and has smaller scope.

6. Avoid single headings. There must be a main topic II to follow the section headed by main topic I; there must be a subtopic B to follow the section headed by subtopic A; and so on.

The following is an example of a topic outline with a title, a thesis statement, and a series of orderly and carefully developed topics.

The Serious Intent of Practical Jokers

Thesis Statement: Practical jokers share four basic motivations: to obtain applause, to feel reassurance, to experience power, and to vent hostility.

- I. Nature of and reasons for practical jokes
    - A. Variety
    - B. Motivations
- II. Applause
    - A. For acting
    - B. For cleverness
- III. Reassurance
    - A. Victim ridiculous
    - B. Joker superior
- IV. Power
    - A. Over joke
    - B. Over victim
- V. Hostility
    - A. Harmless jokes, normal hostility
    - B. Harmful jokes, abnormal hostility
- VI. Practical jokes and human nature

The **sentence outline** represents a more advanced kind of preparation for writing a paper. More thinking has to go into a sentence outline than into a scratch or topic outline, but it is often worth the effort because it offers a tight control over your writing and makes it harder to wander from the subject. As a rule, the more time you spend on your outline, the less time you will need to do the actual writing of the paper. The sentence outline follows the same conventions as the topic outline except that the entries are all expressed in complete sentences. Place periods after sentences in a sentence outline.

The Serious Intent of Practical Jokers

Thesis Statement: Practical jokers share four basic motivations: to obtain applause, to feel reassurance, to experience power, and to vent hostility.

I. The nature of practical jokes differs widely, but the motivations of practical jokers are common to all.
   A. Practical jokes vary from the humorous and harmless to the cruel.
   B. Practical jokers share four basic motivations: to obtain applause, to feel reassurance, to experience power, and to vent hostility.

II. Practical jokers, like most people, crave applause.
   A. They are actors expecting approval of an audience for playing a part well.
   B. They also expect approval for their cleverness.

III. Closely related to the desire for applause is the human need for reassurance.
   A. The practical joker always makes the victim look more or less ridiculous.
   B. By making the victim look silly, the practical joker feels superior.

IV. Practical jokes enable the performer to feel a sense of power.
   A. The joker controls the length and pace of the joke.
   B. Like a puppeteer the joker controls the victim.

V. The practical joker is venting feelings of hostility toward others.
   A. Even jokes which are harmless reflect some degree of hostility in all of us.
   B. Cruel jokes show an abnormal degree of hostility in the performer.

VI. To understand the motivations of practical jokers is to see basic aspects of human nature.

46f Use examples to illustrate generalizations.

Meaningful generalizations frequently rest on illustrations. An abstract truth may become evident only after concrete examples have been given (see **45e**). A string of unillustrated generalizations can make a theme dull and unconvincing. Examples give your paper clarity and color.

Generalization In varying degrees the victim of a practical joke is always made to look ridiculous.

Examples The victim may be tricked into talking into a mailbox where there is a hidden microphone, or slipping on a banana peel, or trying to open a door with a greasy knob.

46g Use the following check list of essentials in writing papers.

Title

The title should accurately suggest the contents of the paper.

It should attract interest without being excessively novel or clever.

It should not be too long.

NOTE   Do not underline the title of your own paper, and do not put quotation marks around it.

Introduction

The introduction should be independent of the title. No pronoun or noun in the opening sentence should depend for meaning on the title.

It should catch the reader's attention.

It should properly establish the tone of the paper as serious, humorous, ironic, or otherwise.

It should include a thesis statement which declares the subject and the purpose directly but at the same time avoids worn patterns like "It is the purpose of this paper to. . . ."

Body

The materials should develop the thesis statement.

The materials should be arranged in logical sequence.

Strong topic sentences (see **45a**) should clearly indicate the direction in which the paper is moving and the relevance of the paragraphs to the thesis statement.

Technical terms should be explained.

Paragraphs should not be choppy.

Enough space should be devoted to main ideas. Minor ideas should be subordinated.

Concrete details should be used appropriately. Insignificant details should be omitted.

Transitions

The connections between sentences and those between paragraphs should be shown by good linking words (see **45g**).

Conclusion

The conclusion should usually contain a final statement of the underlying idea, an overview of what the paper has demonstrated.

The conclusion may require a separate paragraph, but if the paper has reached significant conclusions all along, such a paragraph is not necessary for its own sake.

The conclusion should not merely restate the introduction.

Proofreading

Allow some time, if possible at least one day, between the last draft of the paper and the final finished copy. Then you can examine the paper objectively for wordiness, repetition, incorrect diction, misspellings, faulty punctuation and mechanics, choppy sentences, vague sentences, lack of transitions, and careless errors.

Model Paper

NOTE   If your teacher requires the thesis statement labeled and written in after the title and before the beginning of the paper (as indicated in the following theme), provide it.

The Serious Intent of Practical Jokers

<u>Thesis</u> <u>Statement</u>: Practical jokers share four basic
motivations: to obtain applause, to feel reassurance,
to experience power, and to vent hostility.

Practical jokes vary as much as the people who
indulge in them. Everyone has probably witnessed
numerous harmless and often funny pranks like those
played on April Fool's Day. Other forms of practical
joking, such as those that once characterized college
hazing, are far from humorous. In fact, they can be
sadistically cruel. Even though differences are
evident in their tricks, practical jokers share four
basic motivations: to obtain applause, to feel
reassurance, to experience power, and to vent
hostility. The intensity of these motivations
determines whether the joke is pleasant to all
(including the victim) or only to the practical joker.

In one way or another most people strive for
applause. Practical jokers are in a sense actors.
They desire approval for playing a part well. An
executive who puts a big plastic spider in the chair
of a typist and then with a straight face asks her
what that is beside her loses much of his fun if no
one else is present in the office to see her reaction.
If onlookers are present, they may laugh with him and

thus show their mark of appreciation for his acting.
He feels that they are also saying to him with their
laughter that he is clever and intelligent for
thinking up such a prank, pulling it off so well, and
providing amusement and relief from routine.

Closely related to the desire for applause is the
human need for reassurance. A practical joke is a
reflection of this craving in all of us to make
ourselves look better at someone else's expense. In
varying degrees the victim of a practical joke is
always made to look ridiculous. The victim may be
tricked into talking into a mailbox where there is a
hidden microphone, or slipping on a banana peel, or
trying to open a door with a greasy knob. By making
the victim look silly, the practical joker feels a
momentary flash of superiority. The rational,
composed joker feels superior to the victim, who has
been caught off guard.

Although one may not think of practical jokers as
people who want power, they nevertheless perform their
jokes partly because they are enabled to experience
the thrill of control. They feel power by controlling
the length and pace of the joke itself. They can
hurry it to its conclusion, or they can prolong it and
add refinements as they choose. In a small way,
theirs is the power of creativity. They also

3

experience power over their victim because they are like puppeteers pulling the strings. They are in command; the other person merely responds. They have the advantage because they know what is going on; their victim is in the dark.

Psychologists say that we manifest hostility toward others in dozens of ways that we do not realize. The practical joke offers one of these ways to vent feelings of hostility and aggression in a fashion that is socially acceptable provided the joke is not destructive. The degree of hostility in practical jokers can often be measured by the nature of their pranks. If they send a novice mechanic out for a left-handed wrench, they are probably reflecting the mild hostility that most people feel toward the greenhorns of the world. If, on the other hand, they arrange for the novice to slip on a banana peel on the way and to be hit with a flower pot, their feelings of hostility are probably beyond those of normalcy.

To understand the motivations of practical jokers is to understand something fundamental about human nature. The reasons behind practical jokes may not appear attractive, but they are not in themselves abnormal. Whether we actually perform the jokes or not, we are all practical jokers because in varying degrees we all share the four basic motivations.

Subjects for Papers

Keep a notebook of items which you think may be useful to you as possible subjects and materials for papers. Some possible subjects follow.

Who Should Go to College?	The Center City
Old Photographs	Good Teaching
Suburban Living	The Native American Today
Return to the Country	Television Commercials
Political Cartoons	An Ice Storm
The New Music	Equal Rights for Women
Divorce	The Average Person
The Sports Fan	The Problem of Pollution
Blackness	Good Fences and Good Friends
Patterns of Humor	Educating the Parent
City Folklore	Camping Out
Walking	Parks
A Deserted House	Censorship
Crime	The Subway at Night
Exploring	Credit
The Scientific Attitude	Chicano Culture
The Emergency Ward	Acting in a Play
A Trip Downriver	A Description of a Painting

The following quotations may help you to develop subjects for papers. Support, refute, or use these quotations in any appropriate way. You may think of a subject only remotely related to what the author says.

1. The older generation had certainly pretty well ruined this world before passing it on to us. They give us this Thing, knocked to pieces, leaky, red-hot, threatening to blow up; and then they are surprised that we don't accept it with the same attitude of pretty, decorous enthusiasm with which they received it. . . .   JOHN F. CARTER, JR., "The Overnight Realists"

2. Women, as well as men, can only find their identity in work that uses their full capacities.   BETTY FRIEDAN

3. For generations we have tried to make the world a better place by providing more and more schooling, but so far the endeavor has failed.   IVAN ILLICH, "The Alternative to Schooling"

4. Things are changing in our country, and I am hopeful.
                    MARIAN ANDERSON, *My Lord, What a Morning*

5. No trumpets sound when the important decisions of our life are made. Destiny is made silently. The wheels turn within our hearts for years and suddenly everything meshes and we are lifted to the next level of progress.
                    AGNES DE MILLE, *Dance to the Piper*

6. For there is a cloud on my horizon. A small dark cloud no bigger than my hand. Its name is Progress.
                    EDWARD ABBEY, *Desert Solitaire*

7. The humor in *Peanuts,* then, has a dimension apart from the obvious gag level. This is because the characters in *Peanuts* are reflections of ourselves, and we are funnier than any make-believe character could possible be.
                    MARTIN JEZER, "Quo Peanuts?"

8. The American seems to be becoming more unable to demonstrate the individuality which democracy requires. Continuing hypnotism, emulsification, and homogenization of men by the media is the opposite of what our nation needs. . . .   HARRY J. SKORNIA, "Ratings and Mass Values"

9. We can always judge the value of any piece of literature by the number of genuine emotions or thoughts that it calls forth from us.   MARY ELLEN CHASE

10. The bad dreams of our Utopians will not come true; even the most complex, advanced thinking machine will not replace or dominate this [human] spirit.

JOHN H. TROLL, "The Thinking of Men and Machines"

11. We are not so weak and timorous as to need to be free of fear; we need only use our capacity to not be afraid of it and so relegate fear to its proper perspective.

WILLIAM FAULKNER, "Faith or Fear"

12. Fiction can be "truer" than fact, because it is made up from the observation of hundreds of facts.   ELIZABETH JANEWAY

13. No one can make you feel inferior without your consent.

ELEANOR ROOSEVELT

14. What loneliness is more lonely than distrust?

GEORGE ELIOT (MARY ANN EVANS)

15. Stay, stay at home, my heart, and rest; / Home-keeping hearts are happiest.   HENRY WADSWORTH LONGFELLOW

16. A prophet is not without honor, save in his own country, and in his own house.   MATTHEW 13:57

17. I believe natural beauty has a necessary place in the spiritual development of any individual or any society.

RACHEL CARSON, "A Statement of Belief"

18. To some extent a citizen of any country will feel that the tourist's view of his homeland is a false one.

MARY MCCARTHY, "America the Beautiful"

19. That is happiness; to be dissolved into something complete and great.   WILLA CATHER

20. Our life is frittered away by detail.   THOREAU, *Walden*

21. Ah, one doesn't give up one's country any more than one gives up one's grandmother. HENRY JAMES, *The Portrait of a Lady*

22. Fiction is like a spider's web, attached ever so lightly perhaps, but still attached to life at all four corners.

VIRGINIA WOOLF, *A Room of One's Own*

• *Exercise 7*

Read the three papers that follow, and be prepared to discuss the content and the writing style of each. Be on the lookout for mistakes in spelling, mechanics, grammar, and diction, but pay equal attention to the thought of each essay and the way in which the writer developed it. If you like, give each paper a grade and write a brief paragraph in which you summarize your opinion of the paper. Be prepared to defend your grades and comments.

The Roles of Woman and Man

In my opinion people are too caught up in their ways. Just because something has always been done a certain way people believe it has to keep on being done the same way. I think that attitude is wrong. I believe that the past should not be allowed to control what is going on at the present. I am no expert but in my opinion most people are still afraid to do things any different from the way there parents did it. Not necessarily most people but alot of them.

What can be done about this? One thing that can

be done about this is to look at how people think
either conscious or unconscious about their roles in
life. Take the average woman. In my opinion she has
been so brainwashed that she believes that she cant do
anything but light jobs. She expects, it seems to me,
to have like doors opened for her and she thinks she
has to look after the kids and clean the house and
wash the dirty dishes and not ever do things that
would develope her muscles. A woman has things she is
supposed to do. If she does like do other things she
is put down for being a women's lib.

Men have their roles too. Like they do not feel,
in my opinion, right in taking care of the little ones
and cleaning house and stuff like that, you know.
People have always thought that if the husband stays
home and does the choers and the woman is the bacon
winner, then he must be some kind of a nut or
something. In my opinion that is definately a wrong
attitude. Staying home and washing the dirty dishes,
a contribution can be made by the man just as much as
the woman. Communication is the important thing I
think not roles.

A marriage is not made in heaven. It has to be
worked for. I believe although I admit I have never
been married that alot of romantic noncense has been
written on marriage. This romantic noncense that has
been written puts the woman on a pedastal she is made

to look like a shrinking violent and the man is a
harry chested he man who helps only here and there in
the house. His job is at the factory or ofice. I
don't by any of this. Do whatever you feel like, like
if you want to stay home and wash the dirty dishes and
change the babbies dirty dipers, do it and if the
woman wants to be a police officer thats alright too.

If this goes against the grain and gives you
problems ask who made the rules to begin with? To
begin with the rules were made by people who in my
humbel opinion were narow minded and ignorant.
Why should modern people who are enlighted pay
attention to people from the dark ages who were
puretanical. Do whatever turns you on.

Reading

A wise man once said, "One who is too tired to
read is too tired to breathe." What he meant was
that reading is as important to mankind as life
itself. His exaggeration is excusable, for reading
is, indeed, just about as fundamental to civilized
beings as any other single activity. It is to the
mind what eating is to the body—-sustenance.

But not everyone is civilized. Among us today
are barbarians just as there were at the dawn of time.

It is as difficult to explain the advantages of
reading to these heathens as it is to communicate the
finer points of professional football to someone who
dislikes sports. The joy of silent conversation, the
stimulation of insight, the delight of heightened
imagination--all these advantages are lost to the
automobile mechanic or the plumber who spends his days
in grimy manual labor and his evenings in the inane
world of television or in that haze produced by beer.
Such a person believes that anyone who reads is an
impractical intellectual who is far removed from the
real world. There is no scorn like the scorn of a
non-reader toward a reader.

A recent poll conducted by the Estege Corporation
reveals that seventy-three percent of the people
surveyed on the street could not identify William
Faulkner, perhaps the greatest American novelist of
the twentieth century. One woman seemed to remember
that he was an actor; another believed him to be a
governor of some state. The fate of this land, and
the world besides, is in the hands of a few
intelligent people who can read a book and enjoy it.
The "great unwashed" mass, as it was once called, is
a blight that threatens to spread and destroy
civilization. How can one respect a person who thinks
that existentialism is a rare disease?

The most discouraging aspect of this problem is

that illiteracy, which was once restricted to those
who had little formal schooling, now is creeping up
the educational ladder like a second-story thief on
his way to entering the upper floor of a stately
mansion. Recent results of the College Board
Examinations, administered by the Educational Testing
Service, shows that prospective college students are
making lower and lower scores. Most students who go
to college now hate to read. They consider it a
torture that they must endure in order to receive the
reward of a degree. And the degree is needed so that
they can then become doctors or business executives,
who are more and more resembling the automobile
mechanics, the truck drivers, the carpenters, and the
farmers. They are merely high-class illiterates.
They make more money than the ditchdiggers and
dishwashers, but they are not fundamentally different
because they do not read any more than they have to.
They never pick up Shakespeare or Dickens for the
sheer joy of reading. The poetry of Milton or Chaucer
is as foreign to them as Chinese food to a Frenchman.

If civilization is to continue, it will do so
only because of those who like to read good books.
These few must ban together in mutual appreciation of
the finer things of life and refuse to lower
themselves to the level represented by the news media,
television, and motion pictures. The evangelists of
reading will be scorned, but their cause is just.

46g

A Doctor's Waiting Room

A busy doctor's office offers many various and sundry studies in the human race. A patient comes in, checks in at the receptionist's desk, and sits down in the crowded room. Everyone looks up to study him. He is watched minutely as if he was a rare bird being observed by devoted ornithologists. The other patience seem to wander what his particular medical problem is. They search his face as if they were looking for symptoms. Finally they seem to tire of gazing at him and go back to their magazines he merges into the picture like a pebble sinking into quicksand.

In a few moments, a nurse calls a name as she opens a door into the waiting room. All look up, then all look at the woman who has risen to take her tern with the "doc." She is obviously worried. Her face is drawn and ashen. She appears to be a little bit dizzie as she gets up out of her chair. But she makes it up and goes toward the nurse and gets to the door and when she goes thru the door the nurse, who is hard at work with some chewing gum, speaks to her with an insincere smile: 'How are you today, Miss Emsey.' Miss Emsey replies: "Fine"

Ocassionally a nervous patient tried to make conversation. A beefy woman announced: "Everytime I come I have to wait longer. The woman sitting on her left waits a few seconds, size, and then replies with a sorta frown: "Yes, I know. My husband says that the worse part of going to see the doctor the money is another matter of course is the waiting." They both laugh nervously. While they are carrying on this conversation just mentioned, some of the other patients stare at them in such a way that would be considered rude anywhere else. But for some reason staring is an excepted part of doctor's office ediquite. Soon all go back to turning over the pages of McCall's and old issues of Time and Newsweek.

A middle aged man who is obviously deaf as a doornail comes in and has great difficulty with the receptionist. He is not the least timid at all. She says to him. "May I help you?" He begins to loudly give her his symptoms. They are not nice ones. She is embarrased and hurriedly says: "You will have to explain all that to the doctor." He looks at her for a minute and replies: "What is that you say?" "The doctor," she says, now so loudly that everyone is watching with somewhat of an alarmed look on their various faces, "you'll have to see the doctor." "Well," he shouts back with apparent irritation, "what do you think I'm here for, to apply for a job?" Her face is now scarlet she just points to a chair, and he sits down. She still does not have his name. No one smiles. The receptionist closes the glass

partition and begins to talk to one of the nurses
while she points to the hard of hearing gent. He
sees this going on and thinks it is his time and gets
up and starts into the doctor's office before the
nurse stops him and says, "It will be just a minute,
Mr. Seper." She obviously has dealt with him before.
He goes back and sets down in his chair and grunts.
He has now become the center for all eyes, but still
no one has smiled.

Why does no one smile? There are many reasons.
Some of these reasons might be as follows. Firstly,
folks are not in a smiling mood when they are in a
doctor's office. Secondly, they are not really
themselves. They do smile sometimes, but it is at
things that are not really funny. They smile then
because it is a nervous smile. But when someone is
really a scream like Mr. Seper, don't get me wrong I
really don't mean to put him down or anything like
that then they will not smile. If you have ever spent
any time in a crowded doctor's office I know that you
will agree with me—provided that you are not slanted
—that people are funny!!!

47 Writing About Literature

Literature in its many forms is a representation of life and sometimes a comment on its meaning. In casual readings of literature, students may notice little more than what happens in a

work. Careful students, however, seek to understand the work more thoroughly: they study not only its events and characters but also the way in which the author presents and views them. In reading poetry they examine imagery and other aspects of the poet's craft. Those who attempt to explain a literary work should reveal their own interaction with it in a way that indicates their understanding of the meanings which other readers might not automatically see during a first reading.

47a Choose a work and a precise subject which arouse your interest.

If you have a choice of literary subject, select with care the work and the aspect of it that interests you. Writing a paper about a work which fails to arouse a significant response in you may mean that you will fail to attract the attention of your reader. The good subject should come from the aspect of the work which causes the most precise and intense interaction between you and it. You should find something that you wish to comment about. If the work does not cause that sort of reaction, you may need to choose another work if the assignment allows.

Select a subject appropriate to the length of the assignment. A narrow topic can be significant. Indeed, a short paper on the last paragraph in a novel could provide perspective on the entire novel and perhaps on the literary character of the author.

Although a paper may discuss several topics as they relate to the central point, it should have only one subject, one overall argument to which every paragraph is related. Do not try to cover every aspect of a literary work. Provide focus.

Between the first reading of the literary work and the writing of your paper, you should study in detail every item in the work which relates to your particular topic—the way each part (chapter, paragraph, or stanza) develops the subject, the way character and meanings are revealed, the relationship between the language and the theme, and so on. As you study the work, you should write down in some form every particular idea that might be useful later. After reaching an understanding of some aspect of the work, you should make general notes that will serve as introductions and conclusions to paragraphs and to the entire paper. The very best interpretation of a work of literature may come when it is least expected and when you are not striving for an idea. When the study of the work is completed and all the notes have been taken, much or even most of the paper may be written; and then the main task which remains is to assemble the parts and provide transitions.

47b Give the paper a specific and exact title.

A vague title does not prepare the reader for the paper. A title like "A Criticism of Robert Frost's 'The Ax-Helve' " is virtually meaningless; it is too general because it does not give an indication of the paper's approach to the work. A more exact title might be "Opposing Cultures in Frost's 'The Ax-Helve.' "

47c Give the subject an appropriate kind of development.

A standard method of writing a literary paper is first to announce the topic and then to explain what your methods will be. If you use secondary sources (sources other than the work itself), depending perhaps on the assignment, you should show how your view is different from or similar to previous views (see **48c**). Describe the work or the situation in the work briefly and generally (see **47d; 48a**). Then support your interpretation by citing and quoting and analyzing in the body of the paper. Always make it clear to your reader what you are doing. That is, your reader should have no difficulty knowing when you are stating your thesis, summarizing, paraphrasing (expressing the sense of a passage in your own words), offering proof, analyzing, or concluding. A good paper announces what it will prove, proves it, and then shows the significance of what has been done.

The subject you choose will largely determine the way you write about it. The many kinds of writings about literature fall into several categories. Explanations of a few of the more significant categories follow, with some remarks on special problems.

An interpretation   Most critical papers about literature result from a close study of the work. The writer of an interpretative paper is concerned with identifying literary methods and ideas. Through analyzing the techniques by which these are worked out, the writer presents specific evidence to support the interpretation. Be careful to distinguish between the thinking of a character and that of the author. Unless authors speak for themselves in their own person, you can only deduce from their works as a whole what they think.

A review   A good review should tell precisely what a work attempts to do and what methods it follows in carrying out its aim. If length permits, the review may include a brief outline of the contents. Such information should not be presented for its own sake, however, but as part of the attempt to give a fair and exact view of what the work accomplishes.

A character analysis   Many students seize on the character sketch as an easy kind of critical paper to write. Actually, it is a demanding assignment. The critic accomplishes little by merely summarizing a character's traits and recounting actions without considering motivations, development, and interrelationships with other characters. Alternatively, the critic may choose to describe the method of characterization—*how* the author develops the character. Learn to distinguish between *character* and *characterization.*

A study of setting   Often the time and place in which a work is set suggest something significant about the way places and things interact with people. If you choose to write about setting, you should be able to show how it is more than just a backdrop for the action.

A comparative study   Much can be learned from comparing various facets of two or more works of literature. The purpose of the comparison is the crucial point here. To develop a comparison you must do more than discuss each work in turn. Many good comparative studies use one work to assist in the interpretation of another. Some comparisons reach conclusions that are more general. Two poems may be compared, for example, in such a fashion that the critic can then explain two ways in which poets create images.

Technical analysis   The analysis of technical elements in literature—imagery, symbolism, and so on—requires special study of the technical term or concept as well as of the literary work itself. You might begin by consulting a good basic reference book like C. Hugh Holman's *A Handbook to Literature.* Never use technical or critical terms merely as labels to impress your reader.

Combined approaches   Many papers combine different kinds of approaches. A thoughtful paper on imagery, for example, does more than merely point out the images, or even the kinds of images, in the work under study. Rather, it uses the imagery to interpret or analyze or clarify something else also— theme, structure, characterization, mood, patterns, and so on.

47d Do not summarize and paraphrase excessively.

Tell only as much of the story as is necessary to clarify your interpretations and prove your arguments. Summarizing a plot involves little or no thinking; your thoughts about literature are the crucial measure of your work. When you paraphrase, make it clear that it is the author's thinking which you are reporting, not your own.

47e Think for yourself.

The excellence of your paper will depend finally on the significance of your thinking, your opinion. Do not merely report something you learned *from* the literature; write something you learned *about* it. Spend little or no time telling your reader that it is your belief; it is understood that opinions expressed are your own. Your readers will determine for themselves the importance of your paper according to your accuracy, your evidence, your methods, your thinking. Wild and unsupported thoughts are perhaps worse than pure summary or paraphrase, worse than no thinking at all.

47f Write about the literature, not about yourself or your reading process.

You may be interested in the difference between what you saw in a work on a first reading as opposed to your insights after a second reading, but omit such irrelevant information in your paper. Only your final and considered views should be presented to the reader.

Generally avoid the first person pronouns *I* and *we*. Excessive concern with yourself detracts from what you say about literature and causes irrelevance and wordiness.

47i

47g Provide sufficient evidence to support your points.

A fundamental criterion in the evaluation of a paper is whether it strikes a proper balance between generalization and detailed support. Do not write too abstractly and generally. Make a point; develop its particularities and ramifications; quote the work; and show how your point appears in the quotation. Long quotations are usually not nearly so good as brief quotations followed by analysis and discussion.

Papers, paragraphs, and series of paragraphs usually should not begin with a quotation. A writer who lets someone else start a paper may leave the impression of being lazy and unthoughtful. Paragraphs which conclude with quotations that are not followed by commentary and analysis may also indicate that the writer is leaving much of the thinking to the reader rather than providing sufficient thought.

47h Organize and develop the paper according to significant ideas.

Organizing your paper by the sequence of the story or the poem often results in weaknessess—poor topic sentences, summary rather than thought, mechanical organization, and repetitive transitional phrases. As a rule it is better to go from point to point, idea to idea.

NOTE   Make sure that the title and the early part of your paper together supply the necessary information about the name of the author and the title of the literary work you are discussing.

47i Do not moralize.

Good criticism of literature is not preachy. Avoid the temptation to use your paper as a platform from which to moralize on the rights and wrongs of the world.

Model Paper

Read the following poem by John Keats carefully; then study
the interpretative paper and the explanatory points about it.

La Belle Dame sans Merci

Ah, what can ail thee, wretched wight,
Alone and palely loitering?
The sedge is wither'd from the lake,
And no birds sing.

Ah, what can ail thee, wretched wight,
So haggard and so woe-begone?
The squirrel's granary is full,
And the harvest's done.

I see a lilly on thy brow,
With anguish moist and fever dew;
And on thy cheek a fading rose
Fast withereth too.

I met a lady in the meads
Full beautiful—a faery's child;
Her hair was long, her foot was light,
And her eyes were wild.

I set her on my pacing steed,
And nothing else saw all day long;
For sideways would she lean, and sing
A faery's song.

I made a garland for her head,
And bracelets too, and fragrant zone;
She look'd at me as she did love,
And made sweet moan.

She found me roots of relish sweet,
   And honey wild, and manna dew;
And sure in language strange she said,
   I love thee true.

She took me to her elfin grot,
   And there she gaz'd and sighed deep,
And there I shut her wild sad eyes—
   So kiss'd to sleep.

And there we slumber'd on the moss,
   And there I dream'd, ah woe betide,
The latest dream I ever dream'd
   On the cold hill side.

I saw pale kings, and princes too,
   Pale warriors, death-pale were they all;
They cry'd—"La Belle Dame sans merci
   Hath thee in thrall!"

I saw their starv'd lips in the gloam,
   With horrid warning gaped wide,
And I awoke, and found me here
   On the cold hill side.

And this is why I sojourn here,
   Alone and palely loitering,
Though the sedge is wither'd from the lake,
   And no birds sing.

The first paragraph announces the name of the author and of the poem. A general description of the poem is given, as well as where it is set and what has happened. This introduction gives just enough background for someone who has not read the poem and yet not too much for someone who knows the poem well.

Then the student first tells particularly what the poem is about and in the last of the paragraph states the thesis: that the poem seems to be supernatural but is indeed about an aspect of life that occurs at some time to nearly everyone.

The body of the paper is a contrast between the unnaturalness of the woman and her true human qualities.

The Magic and Reality of Love in Keats's
"La Belle Dame sans Merci"

    John Keats's poem "La Belle Dame sans Merci"
("the beautiful woman without pity") is a sad but
beautiful work about a lover in a world where nature
is dry and weirdly quiet. In winter a horseman
languishes mentally and physically sick by a lake.
The speaker of the poem asks him about his troubles,
and the man tells a story about a love affair which
has made his life not worth living. Keats seems to be
writing a fairy tale which might appeal to anyone, but
he is really telling a story of the unhappiness that
comes from thwarted love. The subject of the poem is
the magical beauties of early love and the horrid
consequences that result when love is gone and one of
the lovers still has not been able to return to the
more customary feelings of everyday life.

    Whatever the nature of the creature the horseman
falls in love with, natural or supernatural, she is
highly desirable in human terms. Yet she seems to be
something more than merely human. The first strange
note is that she was a "faery's child," but any lovely
woman may seem to be magical to an ardent man. The
wildness of her eyes too could be attributed to her
being a normal and beautiful woman. However, her
supernatural qualities are emphasized in the poem, and

Notice how the writer uses brief quotations to analyze and also to prove points.

In this paragraph what seems to be much storytelling and summary at first glance really leads in each instance to a conclusion stated by the interpreter but only hinted at or implied in the poem.

she grows in mystery--a development that could occur either in an ordinary love relationship or in one belonging to a supernatural world. She sings a "faery's song," suggesting the supernatural nature of her mother.

What she discovers for her lover, gives to him, and shows him also suggests the supernatural. The "roots of relish," the "honey wild," and the "manna dew" are delicious foods uncultivated by human beings-- supernatural gifts. The wild man in Coleridge's "Kubla Khan" has fed on "honey-dew." The "manna dew" recalls the manna supernaturally provided by God for the children of Israel in the wilderness. Her very language is strange; it might be merely a dialect foreign to the ears of the horseman, or it might be some kind of supernatural tongue.

The fairy woman takes her lover to an "elfin grot": that is, a place where other weird or supernatural creatures like her dwell. Her home is not a place of this world: it is a cave, underground, away from everyday things. She weeps from her "wild sad eyes," but Keats gives no cause for the crying. She may be a different kind of creature from the man, and she may regret that their relationship cannot be normal or permanent. She lulls the horseman asleep, and he awakes from this unearthly dream to find himself on a "cold hill side" with others who have

Here near the end of the paper the writer describes how Keats uses imagery to show the mind of the horseman.

been enthralled and heartbroken by this beautiful lady without pity. So he sojourns by himself on a hillside where there are no living plants and no singing birds. The poet makes no statement about the length of the spell of suffering or indeed about whether the man will ever recover.

"La Belle Dame sans Merci" may be a poem about a man who falls in love with an unearthly creature who refuses to establish a normal or permanent relation—ship because she is superhuman. On the other hand, the magic may be merely a figure of speech, a vehicle rather than the subject of the poem, an embodiment of the disappointments of any love affair that starts with all the promise of glory and ends with nothing left but the ashes of a burned—out love.

In the end the disappointed lover must face harsh reality. He is pale (a lily is on his brow), but he is sweating with anguish and has a fever. Keats reveals the horseman's disappointed love and his mental state by showing how he looks and feels. The man tells his own story about the magic of his love, and finally he tells of his horrid memories—both dream and reality—and of his pining, sick and by himself. These are the external images of his physical condition which has resulted from his psychological state. Thus at the beginning and the end of the poem the poet presents a picture of a

The conclusion sums up the two skillfully combined but also seemingly contradictory realms of the man's experience with love.

disappointed lover. In between, all the magic of the woman--her beauties, enticements, and general charm-- reflects the joys of what starts out as a requited love.

"La Belle Dame sans Merci" is a poem metaphor- ically about a magical world, but it is about the real world as well. The great accomplishment of the poem is that it is both a poetic story of a magical relationship told with beautiful figures of speech and at the same time a treatment of the harsh truth of actuality.

48 Writing the Research Paper

The research paper is based on a systematic investigation of materials found in a library. This section provides instructions about the way to assemble materials from sources and to document them with footnotes.

48a Choose a subject that interests you. Limit it to manageable size.

Your subject should allow you to use the library extensively, think for yourself, and come to a significant conclusion which will be of interest to your reader. Above all, it should engage your attention so that you enjoy reading and thinking about it and writing it up for others.

Begin by choosing a general subject area. If you have long had a particular interest, it may be your starting point: photography perhaps, or literature, or archaeology, or folklore. If nothing comes to mind, start with a list of broad areas, such as the following, decide on one you like, and then focus on a limited aspect of it.

art	government	industry
music	sociology	science
literature	anthropology	communications
history	economics	medicine
religion	geography	agriculture

At this stage you are trying to relate your investigation to an active interest.

Limit your subject adequately. Suppose you have chosen photography as your general area. After a little thought and reading and a look at the card catalog of the library, you will see that this is too broad a topic for one paper. So you may begin by narrowing it to aerial photography or the history of photography. Any of these topics could be further restricted: for example, "Aerial Photography in World War II" or "Mathew Brady: Photographer of the Civil War." Still further limitation may be desirable, depending on the length of your paper and the resources of your library.

If you are starting with a broad area such as anthropology, history, science, or literature, you may move gradually toward your final subject in a process like the following:

> Anthropology—tribal societies—a tribal people still surviving—American Indians—the Navajo—the lore of the Navajo—Navajo songs.

> Science—one scientific area during a certain period— ecology—nuclear energy and the environment—the controversy surrounding the nuclear plant in the eastern part of the state.

> Literature—the supernatural in literature—science fiction— tales of horror—famous monsters—*Frankenstein.*

In practice, narrowing down from a general to a specific subject is seldom smooth and orderly. Glean ideas for limiting a broad area by skimming an article in an encyclopedia or the subject headings in the card catalog. You may even be well into your preliminary research (see **48b**) before you arrive at the final topic.

As you read and work, consider whether you are trying to cover too much ground or whether, at the other extreme, you are too narrowly confined. If you are not satisfied with your subject after you get into your preliminary reading, try with your teacher's help to work out an acceptable modification of it instead of changing your topic completely.

Avoid inappropriate subjects. Beware of subjects highly technical, learned, or specialized. Only a specialist can handle modern techniques in genetic research or experimental psychology. Some topics, too, may be beyond the scope of the library you will be using. Avoid topics that do not lead to a wide range of source materials. If you find that you are using one or

two sources exclusively, the fault may be with your method—
or with your topic. For example, a process topic (how to do
something) does not lend itself to library investigation. Instead
of writing on "How to Ski," you might study the effect of skiing
on some industry or on some region in the United States.

48b Become acquainted with the reference tools of
the library, and use them to compile a working bibliography.

Certain guides to knowledge are indispensable to library investigation. From them you can compile a **working bibliography,**
a list of published materials which contain information on your
subject and which you plan to read. The items on this list
should have only the author's name, the title, and the information you need in order to find the source in the library.

The basic tool for finding books in the library is the **card
catalog.** Books are listed alphabetically by author, title, and
subject. Catalog cards sometimes refer the reader to additional
subject headings that can suggest new aspects of a topic. Re-
produced on pages 229 and 230 are three typical catalog
cards—actually three copies of the same card filed for different
uses. Notice the typed title and subject headings as well as the
call number typed at the top left. This is the number that tells
where a book can be found on the shelves of the library's collection. Very large libraries and library systems use the Library
of Congress method of classifying materials; smaller libraries
use the Dewey decimal method. The use of author, title, and
subject cards is the same for both.

The card catalog leads you to the books in your library. The
periodicals are indexed in special reference books, which list articles by author, title, and subject. *Readers' Guide to Periodical
Literature* indexes the most widely circulated American periodicals. *The New York Times Index* is described as "The
Master-Key to the News since 1851." There are numerous

48b

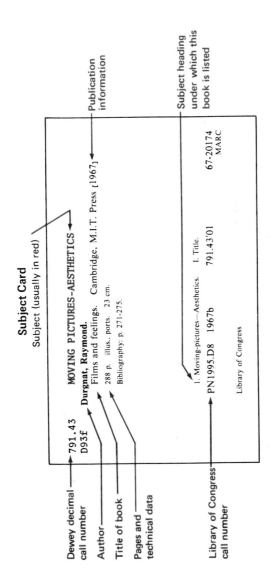

Subject Card
Subject (usually in red)

Dewey decimal call number

791.43
D93f

Author

Title of book

Pages and technical data

MOVING PICTURES—AESTHETICS

Durgnat, Raymond.
Films and feelings.   Cambridge, M.I.T. Press [1967]

288 p.   illus., ports.   23 cm.

Bibliography: p. 271-275.

Publication information

Subject heading under which this book is listed

1. Moving-pictures—Aesthetics.   I. Title.

Library of Congress call number

PN1995.D8   1967b   791.43'01   67-20174
                                                MARC

Library of Congress

Author Card

791.43
D93f

Durgnat, Raymond.
    Films and feelings.   Cambridge, M.I.T. Press [1967]
        288 p. illus., ports. 23 cm.
        Bibliography: p. 271-275.

1. Moving-pictures—Aesthetics.   I. Title.

PN1995.D8   1967b   791.43'01   67-20174

Library of Congress

Title Card

791.43
D93f

Films and feelings.

Durgnat, Raymond.
    Films and feelings.   Cambridge, M.I.T. Press [1967]
        288 p. illus., ports. 23 cm.
        Bibliography: p. 271-275.

1. Moving-pictures—Aesthetics.   I. Title.

PN1995.D8   1967b   791.43'01   67-20174
                                                          MARC

Library of Congress

other periodical indexes of a more specialized or a more scholarly nature. For example, suppose you are writing on Mary Shelley's novel *Frankenstein*. Looking under *Shelley, Mary Wollstonecraft (Godwin)* in the *Social Sciences & Humanities Index,* volume 19, April 1965 to March 1966, you find the following entry:

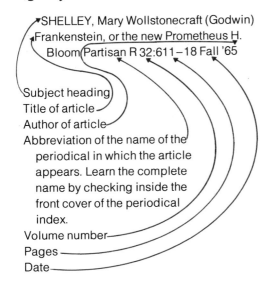

SHELLEY, Mary Wollstonecraft (Godwin)
   Frankenstein, or the new Prometheus H.
      Bloom Partisan R 32:611–18 Fall '65

Subject heading
Title of article
Author of article
Abbreviation of the name of the
   periodical in which the article
   appears. Learn the complete
   name by checking inside the
   front cover of the periodical
   index.
Volume number
Pages
Date

With this information, you should be able to find the article if the periodical is in your library. Of course, you will be unable to read through all the articles written about a broad subject. But you will be able to exclude some merely by studying their titles in the periodical indexes.

Besides using the card catalog and periodical indexes you will want to know about your library's **vertical file,** the cabinet or cabinets containing pamphlets and clipped magazine and newspaper articles that have been filed under subject headings.

Finally, you will also need to know something about standard **reference books.** There are many. The following lists include those you would be likely to find in a large library.

Biographical References

Biography Index
Concise Dictionary of American Biography
Contemporary Authors
Current Biography Yearbook
Kunitz, S., and H. Haycraft, *American Authors, 1600—1900*
Penguin Companion to World Literature
Webster's Biographical Dictionary
Who's Who in America

Encyclopedias

Collier's Encyclopedia
Encyclopaedia Britannica
Encyclopedia Americana
Kane, J. N., *Famous First Facts*
New Century Cyclopedia of Names
The World Book Encyclopedia

Fine Arts

Apel, W., and R. T. Daniel, *The Harvard Brief Dictionary of Music*
Gardner's Art Through the Ages
Janson, H. W., D. J. Janson, and J. Kerman, *A History of Art & Music*
Jordan, R. F., *A Concise History of Western Architecture*
Murray, P. and L., *Dictionary of Art and Artists*
Penguin Dictionary of Architecture
Pollack, P., *The Picture History of Photography*
The Praeger Picture Encyclopedia of Art
Scholes, P., *The Oxford Companion to Music*

Geography and Atlases

The American Heritage Pictorial Atlas of United States History
Goode's World Atlas
National Geographic Atlas of the World
Shepherd, W. R., *Historical Atlas*
Webster's Geographical Dictionary
Worldmark Encyclopedia of the Nations

Language

Acronyms & Initialisms Dictionary
The American Heritage Dictionary of the English Language
Funk & Wagnalls Modern Guide to Synonyms and Related Words
Funk & Wagnalls Standard College Dictionary
Morris, W., *Harper Dictionary of Contemporary Usage*
Morris, W. and M., *Dictionary of Word and Phrase Origins*
The New American Roget's College Thesaurus in Dictionary Form
The Random House College Dictionary
Strunk, W., and E. B. White, *The Elements of Style*
Webster's New Collegiate Dictionary
Webster's New World Dictionary of the American Language
Webster's Third New International Dictionary
Wentworth, H., and S. Flexner, *Dictionary of American Slang*

Literature

Cassell's Encyclopedia of World Literature
Granger's Index to Poetry and Recitations
Hart, J. D., *The Oxford Companion to American Literature*
Holman, C., *A Handbook to Literature*
The Reader's Encyclopedia
Sampson, G., *Concise Cambridge History of English Literature*
Spiller, R. E., and others, *Literary History of the United States*

Stevenson, B., *The Home Book of Quotations*
Stevenson, B., *The Macmillan Book of Proverbs, Maxims, and Famous Phrases*

Science and Mathematics

Compton's Dictionary of the Natural Sciences
James & James Mathematics Dictionary
The Larousse Encyclopedia of Animal Life
Life Nature Library
Life Science Library
Penguin Dictionary of Science
The Peterson Field Guide Series
Science Year; the World Book Science Annual
Van Nostrand's Scientific Encyclopedia

Social Science and History

Dunan, M., *Larousse Encyclopedia of Ancient and Medieval History*
Dunan, M., *Larousse Encyclopedia of Modern History*
Great Ages of Man
Greenwald, D., and others, *McGraw-Hill Dictionary of Modern Economics*
Langer, W. L., *An Encyclopedia of World History*
The Statesman's Year-Book
Statistical Abstract of the United States
The World Almanac and Book of Facts

Your working bibliography should grow as you proceed. Be sure to include all the information that will help you find each item listed: along with the author and title, you will need the library call number for books, and the date, volume, and page numbers for articles.

48c Distinguish between primary and secondary materials.

Primary materials are such things as a painting, a poem, a short story, a motor, a stock exchange, an animal, a fossil, a virus, or a public opinion poll. In a paper on gasolines, for example, the gasolines tested are primary materials; the writings of engineers about them are secondary. Primary materials for a study of tourists abroad would consist of published and unpublished diaries, journals, and letters by tourists; interviews with tourists; and anything that is part of the tourist's life. If possible, try to select a topic which allows use of some primary materials so that you can reach independent conclusions and not rely entirely on the thinking of others.

  Secondary materials are those written *about* your topic. In a study of tourists abroad, for example, the writings of journalists and historians about them are called secondary sources. The significance and accuracy of such materials should be evaluated. It is important to consider when a work was written; what information was available to its author at that time; the general scholarly reputation of the author; the extent of the author's knowledge and reliability as indicated in the preface, footnotes, or bibliography; the logic the author has demonstrated in proving points; and even the medium of publication. A general article in a popular magazine, for example, is likely to be less reliable than a scholarly article in a learned journal.

48d Locate source materials, read, evaluate, and take notes.

Before you begin to take notes, it is a good idea to do some broad **preliminary reading** in an encyclopedia or in other general introductory works. Try to get a general view, a kind of map of the territory within which you will be working.

After you have compiled a working bibliography **(48b),** located some of the sources you wish to use, and done some preliminary reading, you are ready to begin collecting specific material for your paper. If you are writing a formally documented paper, make a **bibliography card** for each item as you examine it. This will be a full and exact record of bibliographical information, preferably on a 3 × 5 inch index card. From these cards you will later compile a final bibliography for your paper. A sample card is shown on page 237. The essential information includes the name of the author, the title of the work, the place and date of publication, and the name of the publisher. If the work has an editor or a translator, is in more than one volume, or is part of a series, these facts should be included. For magazine or newspaper articles, the author, title, and name of the publication should be recorded, along with the date and page numbers. For later checking, record the library call number.

For **note-taking,** your next step, use another set of index cards. Develop the knack of skimming so that you can move quickly over irrelevant material and concentrate on pertinent information. Use the table of contents, the section headings, and the index to find chapters or pages of particular use to you. As you read and take notes, consider what subtopics you will use. The two processes work together: your reading will give you ideas for subtopics, and the subtopics will give direction to your note-taking. At this point you are already in the process of organizing and outlining the paper. Suppose you wish to make a study of Mary Shelley's novel *Frankenstein.* You might work up the following list of tentative topics:

Mary Shelley's background
Stage and film versions of *Frankenstein*
Modern concept of the term "Frankenstein"
Mary Shelley's social philosophy
Frankenstein's tragic flaw
The quality of horror in *Frankenstein*

Bibliography Card
(reduced facsimile — actual size 3″ × 5″)

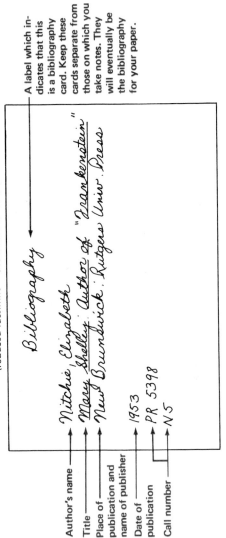

A label which in-
dicates that this
is a bibliography
card. Keep these
cards separate from
those on which you
take notes. They
will eventually be
the bibliography
for your paper.

Bibliography

Nitchie, Elizabeth
Mary Shelley: Author of "Frankenstein."
New Brunswick: Rutgers Univ. Press
1953
PR 5398
N5

Author's name
Title
Place of
publication and
name of publisher
Date of
publication
Call number

These headings may not be final. You should always be ready to delete, add, and change headings as you read and take notes. At this stage, the final order of headings—the outline—may be neither possible nor necessary.

To illustrate the methods of note-taking, suppose you have found the following paragraph about Mary Shelley.

> Mary had been well trained in liberal thought. She had been brought up in the household of the author of *Political Justice.* . . . She had early imbibed ideas of the superfluousness, in a reasonable and benevolent society, of positive institutions. When the many were great and good, there would result an ideal world whose foundations would be political freedom and a social order based on equality and justice.
>
> ELIZABETH NITCHIE, *Mary Shelley:*
> *Author of "Frankenstein"*

You may make a note on this passage by paraphrasing, by quoting, or by combining short quotations with paraphrasing.

To **paraphrase** is to express the sense of a passage entirely in your own words, selecting and summarizing only information and ideas that will be useful. The card on page 239 identifies the source, gives a subject heading, indicates the page number, and then records relevant information in the student's own words. It *extracts* items of information instead of merely recasting the entire passage and line of thought in different words. Notice the careful selection of details and the fact that the paraphrase is considerably shorter than the original.

If at the time of taking notes you cannot yet determine just what information you wish to extract, you may copy an entire passage. For later reference you must then be careful to show by quotation marks that it is copied word for word.

When writing your paper, you may either quote directly or paraphrase. Except for the ellipsis (see **28c**), the note at the top of page 240 went directly from book to card.

48d

Paraphrased Notes

(reduced facsimile — actual size 3″ × 5″)

Subject heading ────────▶ Mary Shelley's social thought

Identification of source ──▶ Nitchie, Mary Shelley
Full bibliographical
information has been
taken down on the
bibliography card.

Page number ────────▶ 35 Mary Shelley, largely because
of her family background, believed
that social institutions would
be unnecessary when people
accepted one another benevolently
and equally.

Quotation

> Mary Shelley's social thought
>
> Nitchie
> 35 "Mary had been well trained in liberal thought. She had been brought up in the household of the author of Political Justice.... She had early imbibed ideas of the superfluousness, in a reasonable and benevolent society, of positive institutions."

Quotation and Paraphrase

> Mary Shelley's social thought
>
> Nitchie
>
> 35 Mary Shelley was born into a family of liberal thinkers. Even when young she developed the idea of the "superfluousness, in a reasonable and benevolent society, of positive institutions."

Short quotations and paraphrasing may be combined on a single note card, as shown on page 240. It is most important to use quotation marks accurately when writing the note, to use your own words when not quoting, and to transfer quotations and quotation marks from card to paper with scrupulous care.

Any single card should contain notes from only one source, and all the notes on any single card should be about one single subject, such as Mary Shelley's social thought, shown on the preceding cards. This will give you maximum flexibility in organizing materials as the plan of the paper takes shape. Arrange the cards by topic before you write the paper.

The accuracy of your paper depends to a great extent on the accuracy of your notes. Indicate on each card the source, the page numbers, and an appropriate subject heading.

Note-taking is not a mere mechanical process; it involves interpretation and evaluation. Two persons writing on the same subject and using the same sources would not be likely to take quite the same notes, and their papers would differ accordingly in content and organization.

Study the following passage, which deals with the 1931 film about Frankenstein. Assume that you are writing a paper on that subject, and decide what kind of notes you would take.

> Florey was responsible for the plot twist whereby the Monster is given a madman's brain, hence betraying the author's original intention. Mary Shelley's tale tells of a scientist who creates a monster, a hideously misshapen creature, harmless at first but soon driven to commit murder and perform other acts of terror through the fear and revulsion his appearance provokes in others. The movie Monster is a murderous fiend, devoid (at least in this first appearance) of reason and barely glimpsed as a human during the episode of the child who befriends him and whom he gratuitously drowns in a lake. This scene with the little girl, incidentally, was the only one to be deleted after audience reaction proved too violently adverse.   CARLOS CLARENS, *An Illustrated History of the Horror Films*

Quotation

The novel and the film

Clarens, *Horror Films*
63 "Florey was responsible for the
plot twist whereby the Monster is
given a madman's brain, hence
betraying the author's original
intention.... The movie Monster
is a murderous fiend, devoid ... of
reason and barely glimpsed as
human...."

Audience response to film

Clarens, *Horror Films*
63 "... the child who befriends
him ... he [the Monster] gratuitously
drowns in a lake. This scene ...,
incidentally, was the only one
to be deleted after audience
reaction proved too violently
adverse."

Paraphrase

Mary Shelley's Monster

Clarens, <u>Horror Films</u>
63 Unlike the film Monster,
the creature in Mary Shelley's
novel is made to commit his
violent acts because he is
rejected by others.

Quotation and Paraphrase

Mary Shelley's Monster

Clarens, <u>Horror Films</u>
63 In the film "the Monster is
given a madman's brain, hence
betraying the author's original
intention." In the novel the
Monster is "driven to commit
murder" because others react to
him with "fear and revulsion."

From a passage as full of information as this one, it is possible to take several kinds of notes under different subject headings. Most of this material might eventually be used in a paper, but to a certain extent the material is adapted to the purposes of the paper by the way it is selected and classified under the student's subject headings. By the very process of reading and note-taking, students think about the subject and organize their thoughts. This is the supreme importance of taking notes, of quoting and paraphrasing. Now study the notes on pages 242–243, all from the preceding paragraph by Clarens. Observe the variety in subject headings and treatment.

48e Construct an outline.

As you read and take notes, think constantly about the organization of your paper. Revise subject headings; experiment with different ways of arranging your topics and your notes; study your notes to detect gaps in evidence or weaknesses in interpretation.

Your note cards should now be grouped by subject headings. Try to put the groups in the order in which you will present your material in your paper. You may shuffle the cards many times before you arrive at an order that satisfies you, and you may yet rearrange some topics during the process of writing. See the model outline on page 249.

48f Acknowledge your sources. Avoid plagiarism.

Acknowledge your indebtedness to others by giving full details of sources in footnotes and bibliography. Using others' words and ideas as if they were your own is a form of stealing called plagiarism.

Some of the principles of quoting and paraphrasing have already been discussed under the topic of taking notes (**48d**).

They must be kept in mind during the writing and revision of the paper. Finally, quotations and paraphrases should be carefully checked for accuracy after the paper is written.

All direct quotations must be placed in quotation marks and acknowledged in your text. If you are writing a documented paper, specific details of the citation must be completed in a footnote (see pages 246–247). Even when you take only a phrase or a single unusual word from a passage, you should enclose it in quotation marks. You may quote words, phrases, clauses, sentences, or even whole paragraphs. Generally you should quote a sentence or a paragraph only when a writer has phrased something especially well and when you need to supply all the information given. Do not quote too much. A sequence of quotations strung together with a few words of your own is not satisfactory. Excessive quoting indicates that you have not properly digested your sources, thought about the ideas, and learned to express them in your own words and to relate them to your own ideas.

All paraphrases and citations must be acknowledged. Credit a source when you cite ideas or information from it even when you do not quote directly. Altering the wording does not make the substance yours. An acknowledgment not only gives proper credit but also lends authority to your statement. Whenever you consult a source or a note card as you write, you are probably paraphrasing, and you probably need an acknowledgment.

In paraphrasing you are expressing the ideas of another writer in your own words. A good paraphrase preserves the sense of the original, but not the form. It does not retain the sentence patterns and merely substitute synonyms for the original words, nor does it retain the original words and merely alter the sentence patterns. It is a genuine restatement. Invariably it should be briefer than the source. In the following example, notice the difference between a satisfactory and an unsatisfactory paraphrase:

Original Hemingway's debt to journalism was a large one, and he always acknowledged it. Unlike many ex-journalists, however, he neither sentimentalized the profession nor misunderstood its essential threat to creative writing. CHARLES A. FENTON, *The Apprenticeship of Ernest Hemingway*

Badly Paraphrased Hemingway's indebtedness to journalism was very great, and he himself said so. Unlike so many writers who have done newspaper work, however, he did not sentimentalize journalism or misunderstand that it is a danger to creative talent.

Better Hemingway admitted that he learned from newspaper work. But he also recognized that journalism can hurt writers as well as help them.

If the source has stated the idea more concisely than you can, you should quote, not paraphrase.

Do not make use of extended paraphrases. If a good many of your paragraphs are simply long paraphrases, your reader will assume that even your organization is taken from someone else. The reader will conclude that you have not assimilated your materials and thought independently about them—that you have not done an acceptable piece of original work.

48g Follow accepted practices of documentation.

Although there is common agreement on the *principles* of documentation, the *forms* vary. The entries that follow may serve you as models, though your teacher may suggest or require modifications.

Sample Footnotes

Reference to a book

¹ Henry Nash Smith, *Mark Twain: The Development of a Writer* (Cambridge: Harvard University Press, 1962), p. 83.

2 Kai-yu Hsu and Helen Palubinskas, eds., *Asian-American Authors,* 2nd ed. (Boston: Houghton Mifflin, 1976), p. 113.

NOTE   First names and *Company* are often omitted from the names of publishers.

Reference to a magazine article

3 Herman J. Viola, "How *did* an Indian chief really look?" *Smithsonian,* June 1977, p. 100.

NOTE   For a weekly or monthly magazine the complete date may be given in place of the volume number; the page number is always supplied.

Later reference to a book or magazine article

4 Smith, p. 81.

Reference to an unsigned encyclopedia article

5 "Midway Islands," *Encyclopedia Americana,* 1977 ed.

Reference to an unsigned newspaper article

6 "Churchill's Account of His Early Wars Is Ridiculed in a Contemporary's Notes," *New York Times,* 23 July 1972, p. 12.

NOTE   When an article is signed, the author's name should be given at the beginning of the footnote.

Reference to a pamphlet

7 Nancy Doyle, *Woman's Changing Place: A Look at Sexism,* Public Affairs Pamphlet No. 509 (New York: Public Affairs Committee, Inc., 1974), p. 4.

Sample Bibliographical Entries

A bibliography should include all the materials referred to in the footnotes for the paper. The items are listed in alphabetical order. Page numbers should be supplied for those works read only in part. The following sample entries cover only the most frequently used types of works.

"Churchill's Account of His Early Wars Is Ridiculed in a Contemporary's Notes." *New York Times,* 23 July 1972, p. 12.

Doyle, Nancy. *Woman's Changing Place: A Look at Sexism.* Public Affairs Pamphlet No. 509. New York: Public Affairs Committee, Inc., 1974.

Hsu, Kai-yu, and Helen Palubinskas, eds. *Asian-American Authors,* 2nd ed. Boston: Houghton Mifflin, 1976, pp. 113–122.

"Midway Islands," *Encyclopedia Americana,* 1977 ed.

Smith, Henry Nash. *Mark Twain: The Development of a Writer.* Cambridge: Harvard University Press, 1962.

————. *Virgin Land: The American West as Symbol and Myth.* Cambridge: Harvard University Press, 1950.

NOTE   The dash takes the place of repeating the author's name.

Viola, Herman J. "How *did* an Indian chief really look?" *Smithsonian,* June 1977, pp. 100–104.

Model Research Paper

A research paper should have ample, even margins and double-spaced text. If you type the paper, indent five spaces for paragraphs. Leave two spaces after periods and other terminal punctuation, and leave one space after other marks of punctuation.

The title page should consist of the title and your name, along with any other information—such as the name of the course or the date—that your teacher wishes to have supplied. If your teacher tells you to submit an outline with your paper, it should occupy a separate, unnumbered page following the title page and should follow the form for the outline illustrated in **46e.**

An outline and the first two pages of a research paper, with accompanying explanations, are given on the following pages for study.

48g

Frankenstein's Lonely Monster

THESIS STATEMENT: An examination of **Mary** Shelley's
<u>Frankenstein</u> reveals a novel with a strong moral and
social theme, the need for human fellowship.

    I. Versions of the story of Frankenstein

        A. The novel

        B. Later plays and motion pictures

        C. Common meaning of term "Frankenstein"

            1. Derivation of popular concept

            2. Difference between popular concept and
                theme of novel

   II. Background of Mary Shelley's social thought

        A. Mary Wollstonecraft and women's rights

        B. William Godwin's social philosophy

 III. Creation of monster and Frankenstein's response

        A. Monster's moral sense and early tendencies

        B. Frankenstein's revulsion

  IV. Horror of loneliness

        A. Importance of loneliness as theme

        B. Robert Walton's search for companionship

        C. Monster's loneliness

            1. His plea for acceptance

            2. Nature of relationship with Frankenstein

            3. His grief over Frankenstein's death

        D. Frankenstein's isolation

   V. Frankenstein's tragic flaw

        A. His failure to love

        B. Mary Shelley's indictment of society

Center the title on the page. Triple-space between the title and the first line of text.

The first paragraph here provides exposition, information that readers must have before they can understand the thesis statement and direction of the paper. After identifying the novel and the author, the paper tells how the adaptations of the original have created their own meanings of the scientist and the monster. Then in the last sentence of the paragraph, the paper gets back to the novel itself and provides direction and purpose with a strong thesis statement.

Place footnote numbers slightly above the line of type and after marks of punctuation. Do not place a period after the number. Number footnotes consecutively throughout the paper.

Separate footnotes from the text by a short ruled line starting at the left-hand margin and placed far enough below the last line of the text so that it will not be mistaken for underlining to indicate italics.

Indent the first line of every footnote five spaces; do not indent succeeding lines.

In footnotes (but not in the bibliography) the author's name is written in normal order, first name first.

Footnote 1 shows one way of referring to an article in a periodical; it also shows how to refer to a book.

Footnote 2 refers the interested reader to further material on the most famous film version of *Frankenstein*. Footnotes of this kind include information not directly relevant to the main subject of the paper but closely enough related to warrant mention in a footnote. Note particularly the form of a reference to a weekly periodical.

The page number for the first page may be omitted or centered at the bottom.

Frankenstein's Lonely Monster

Frankenstein, or the Modern Prometheus (1818) was
written by nineteen-year-old Mary Wollstonecraft
Shelley, the daughter of brilliant parents and the
wife of a major poet, Percy Bysshe Shelley. Almost
from the time of the novel's publication, Victor
Frankenstein and his horrible monster have been the
subjects of dozens of plays and, in the twentieth
century, scores of motion pictures.[1] Most of them
have two ingredients in common. They tend to make
Victor Frankenstein a cold, inhuman scientist, and
they portray the monster as a conscienceless,
uncontrollable killer (with the diseased brain of a
criminal), who grunts his way from one murder to
another.[2] Mainly because of these popular and highly
sensational versions of Mary Shelley's novel,
"Frankenstein" has become a household word, "a synonym
for a man whose own works bring him to disaster or
destruction. And as the monster . . . bears no name,

---

[1] See Elizabeth Nitchie, "The Stage History of
Frankenstein," South Atlantic Quarterly, 41 (1942),
pp. 384-98, and Ivan Butler, The Horror Film (New
York: A. S. Barnes, 1967), pp. 40-45.

[2] The most famous and influential of all motion
pictures about Frankenstein starred Boris Karloff as
the monster. When it appeared in December, 1931, in
New York, one reviewer commented that the monster
communicated its anger and frustration by "squeaking
and grunting" ("Frankenstein," Time, 14 Dec. 1931,
p. 25). See Carlos Clarens, An Illustrated History of
the Horror Films (New York: Putnam's, 1967), pp.
62-65; Raymond Durgnat, Films and Feelings (Cambridge: M.I.T. Press, 1967), p. 106; and Pauline Kael,
Kiss Kiss Bang Bang (Boston: Little, Brown, 1968),
p. 148.

Place the page number in the upper right-hand corner, two lines above the first line of text. Use Arabic numerals; do not put a period after the number.

To place special emphasis upon these words, which will be used again later in the paper, the student has underlined them. The writer must indicate when this is done.

When ellipsis points are used to indicate omitted words at the end of a sentence, the three periods are preceded by a fourth.

Footnote 3 illustrates the standard form for a signed article in an encyclopedia.

Footnotes are used not only to give readers further references to read and to lead them to the sources used in the paper, but also to aid in developing the argument by giving evidence or examples, as footnote 5 illustrates.

Footnote 6 illustrates a reference to the editor's introduction to a work by another writer.

48g

2

the name of his creator has been often transferred to
him so that 'a Frankenstein' has come to signify, in
popular usage, a being of the most appalling ugliness
and brutality, _having no trace of the moral sense
whatever_" (italics mine).[3] This modern concept of
Frankenstein and his monster differs widely from the
original. An examination of Mary Shelley's novel
reveals a book with a strong moral and social theme,
the need for human fellowship.

It was no accident that Mary Shelley should
stress this social ideal in her first novel. She was
nurtúred on the principles of equality. Her mother,
Mary Wollstonecraft Godwin, was a vigorous campaigner
for women's rights.[4] Mrs. Godwin's most notable book,
A Vindication of the Rights of Woman (1792), is a bold
and brilliant plea for equality.[5] In it she "points
out that among 'unequals there can be no society.'
She insists on this condition of equality for all
mankind. . . ."[6]

---

[3] Wilbur L. Cross, "Frankenstein," _Encyclopedia
Americana_, 1964 ed.

[4] See Ralph M. Wardle, _Mary Wollstonecraft: A
Critical Biography_ (Lawrence: University of Kansas
Press, 1951), and Elizabeth Robins Pennell, _Mary
Wollstonecraft Godwin_ (London: Allen, 1885).

[5] Mary Shelley did not know her mother, who died
when Mary was born. However, she was well acquainted
with Mary Godwin's writings and shared many of her
ideas.

[6] Charles W. Hagelman, Jr., "Introduction," _A
Vindication of the Rights of Woman_, by Mary Wollstonecraft (New York: Norton, 1967), p. 16.

Bibliographical Form

The following page shows the bibliography that accompanies the model research paper. Below are guidelines for the preparation of a bibliography.

1. Start the bibliography on a new page as the last section of your paper. Head the page Bibliography, centered. Triple-space below the heading.

2. Do not indent the first line of an entry; indent succeeding lines five spaces.

3. Double-space between entries; single-space within an entry.

4. List only those sources actually used in your paper and referred to in footnotes.

5. Authors are listed with surnames first. If a book has more than one author, however, the names of authors after the first one are put in normal order.

6. List entries alphabetically. When more than one book by the same author is listed, use a long dash (about one inch) in place of the author's name in entries after the first. An entry without an author (for example, an unsigned magazine article) is listed alphabetically by the first word.

7. List the inclusive pages of articles.

8. Notice that the important divisions of entries are separated by periods.

9. A bibliographical entry should include all the information that will enable readers to find the source readily if they wish to do so.

Bibliography

Bloom, Harold. "Frankenstein, or the New Prometheus."
    Partisan Review, 32 (1965), pp. 611–18.

Brailsford, H. N. Shelley, Godwin, and Their Circle.
    New York: Holt, n.d.

Butler, Ivan. The Horror Film. New York: A. S.
    Barnes, 1967.

Clarens, Carlos. An Illustrated History of the
    Horror Films. New York: Putnam's, 1967.

Cross, Wilbur L. "Frankenstein." Encyclopedia
    Americana, 1964 ed.

Durgnat, Raymond. Films and Feelings. Cambridge,
    Mass.: M.I.T. Press, 1967.

"Frankenstein." Time, 14 Dec. 1931, p. 25.

Goodwin, William. Caleb Williams. Ed. David
    McCracken. London: Oxford University Press,
    1970.

Goldberg, M. A. "Moral and Myth in Mrs. Shelley's
    Frankenstein." Keats–Shelley Journal, 8 (1959),
    pp. 27–38.

Kael, Pauline. Kiss Kiss Bang Bang. Boston: Little,
    Brown, 1968.

Lund, Mary Graham: "Mary Godwin Shelley and the
    Monster." University of Kansas City Review, 28
    (1962), pp. 253–58.

Milton, John. The Works of John Milton. 18 vols.
    Ed. Frank Allen Patterson et al. New York:
    Columbia University Press, 1931–1938.

Nitchie, Elizabeth. Mary Shelley: Author of "Franken-
    stein," New Brunswick: Rutgers University Press,
    1953.

_____. "The Stage History of Frankenstein." South
    Atlantic Quarterly, 41 (1942), pp. 384–98.

Pennell, Elizabeth Robins. Mary Wollstonecraft
    Godwin. London: Allen, 1885.

Shelley, Mary Wollstonecraft. Frankenstein, or the
    Modern Prometheus. Ed. M. K. Joseph. London:
    Oxford University Press, 1969.

Shelley, Percy Bysshe. The Complete Works of Percy
    Bysshe Shelley. 10 vols. Ed. Roger Ingpen and
    Walter E. Peck New York: Scribner's, 1926–1930.

Smith, Elton Edward, and Esther Greenwell Smith.
    <u>William Godwin</u>. Twayne's English Authors Series.
    New York: Twayne, 1965.

Wardle, Ralph M. <u>Mary Wollstonecraft</u>: <u>A Critical
    Biography</u>. Lawrence: University of Kansas Press,
    1951.

Wollstonecraft, Mary. <u>A Vindication of the Rights of
    Woman</u>. Ed. Charles W. Hagelman, Jr. New York:
    Norton, 1967.

Glossary of Usage and Terms

49 Glossary

Many items not listed here are covered in other sections of this book and may be located through the index. For words and terms found neither in this glossary nor in the index, consult an up-to-date dictionary. The usage labels (*informal, nonstandard,* and so on) affixed to words in this glossary reflect the opinions of two or more of the dictionaries listed on page 134.

A, an Use *a* as an article before consonant sounds; use *an* before vowel sounds.

a nickname	*an* office
a house	*an* hour
(The *h* is sounded.)	(The *h* is not sounded.)
a historical novel	
(Some speakers say *an.*)	
a union	*an* uncle
(Long *u* has the consonant sound of *y.*)	

Absolute phrase   A noun followed by a modifier; the phrase modifies the sentence as a whole.

Her job finished, she went home.

Accept, except   As a verb, *accept* means "to receive"; *except* means "to exclude." *Except* as a preposition means "but."

Every legislator *except* Mr. Whelling refused to *accept* the bribe.

We will *except* (exclude) this novel from the list of those to be read.

Accidently   A misspelling usually caused by mispronunciation. Use *accidentally.*

Ad   Informal; a clipped form of *advertisement.*

Adapt, adopt   *Adapt* means "to adjust." *Adopt* means "to take up and use as one's own."

The child *adapted* to her new environment.
The laboratory *adopted* a new procedure.

Adjective   A word which modifies a noun or a pronoun. See **10**.

The young horse jumped over *a high* barrier for *the first* time.

Adjective clause   See **Dependent clause**.

Adverb   A word which modifies a verb, an adjective, or another adverb. See **10**.

Adverbial clause   See **Dependent clause**.

Advice, advise   Use *advice* as a noun, *advise* as a verb.

Affect, effect   *Affect* is usually a verb meaning "to act upon" or "to influence." *Effect* may be a verb or a noun. *Effect* as a verb means "to cause" or "to bring about"; *effect* as a noun means "a result," "a consequence."

49

The patent medicine did not *affect* (influence) the disease.

The operation did not *effect* (bring about) an improvement in the patient's health.

The drug had a drastic *effect* (consequence) on the speed of the patient's reactions.

Aggravate Informal in the sense of "annoy," "irritate," or "pester." Formally, it means "to make worse or more severe."

Agree to, agree with *Agree to* a thing (plan, proposal); *agree with* a person.

He *agreed to* the insertion of the plank in the platform of the party.

She *agreed with* the senator that the plank would not gain many votes.

Ain't Nonstandard.

All ready, already *All ready* means "prepared," "in a state of readiness"; *already* means "before some specified time" or "previously" and describes an action that is complete.

The hunters were *all ready* to start. (fully prepared)

Mr. Bowman had *already* bagged his limit of quail. (action completed at time of statement).

All together, altogether *All together* describes a group as acting or existing collectively; *altogether* means "wholly," "entirely."

The sprinters managed to start *all together*.

She does not *altogether* approve the decision.

Allusion, illusion An *allusion* is a casual reference. An *illusion* is a false or misleading sight or a mistaken belief.

Alot Always write as two words. See **Lot of, lots of.**

Alright   Not standard spelling for *all right.*

A.M., P.M.   Used only with figures, as in "6:00 P.M."

Not   The wreck occurred this A.M.
But   The wreck occurred this morning.

Among, between   *Among* is used with three or more persons or things; *between* is used with only two.

It will be hard to choose *between* the two candidates.

It will be hard to choose *among* so many candidates.

Amount, number   *Amount* refers to mass or quantity; *number* refers to things which may be counted. *Amount* refers to a singular word, *number* to a plural.

That is a large *number* of turtles for a pond which has such a small *amount* of water.

An   See **A.**

And etc.   The *and* is unnecessary. See **Etc.**

Antecedent   A word to which a pronoun refers.

antecedent   pronoun

When the ballet *dancers* appeared, *they* were dressed in pink.

Anyways   Not considered standard; use *anyway.*

Anywheres   Not considered standard; use *anywhere.*

Appositive   A word, phrase, or clause used as a noun and placed beside another word to explain it.

appositive

The poet *John Milton* wrote *Paradise Lost* while he was blind.

Around   Informal for *about.*

Article   *A* and *an* are indefinite articles; *the* is the definite article.

As   Weak in the sense of *because:*

The client collected the full amount of insurance, *as* his car ran off the cliff and was totally demolished.

Auxiliary verb   A verb used to help another verb indicate tense, mood, or voice. Principal auxiliaries are forms of the verbs *to be, to do,* and *to have.*

I *am* studying.
I *was* told to be ready by noon.
I *do* not think so.
I *shall* be there next week.
She *has* found a job.

Awful   A trite and feeble substitute for such words as *bad, shocking,* and *ugly.*

Awhile, a while   *Awhile* is an adverb; *a while* is an article and a noun.

Stay *awhile.*

Wait here for *a while.*

Bad, badly   See **10c**.

Because   See **Reason is because**.

Being as, being that   Use *because* or *since.*

Beside, besides   *Beside* means "by the side of," "next to"; *besides* means "in addition to."

Mr. Potts was sitting *beside* the stove.

No one was in the room *besides* Mr. Potts.

Between   See **Among**.

49

Between you and I   Wrong case (see **9b**); use *between you and me.*

Bring, take   *Bring* denotes motion toward the speaker. *Take* denotes motion away from the speaker.

Not   *Bring* the saw to her.

But   *Bring* me the hammer, and *take* the saw to her.

Bust, busted   Slang as forms of *burst. Bursted* is also unacceptable.

Can, may   In formal English *can* is still used to denote ability; *may,* to denote permission. Informally, the two are interchangeable.

Formal   *May* (not *can*) I go?

Can't hardly, can't help but   See **Double negative.**

Capital, capitol   *Capitol* designates "a building which is a seat of government"; *capital* is used for all other meanings.

Case   English has remnants of three cases: subjective (nominative), possessive, and objective. Nouns are inflected (changed in form) for case only in the possessive *(father, father's).* An alternative way to show possession is with an *of* phrase *(the house, of the house).* Some pronouns, notably the personal pronouns *(I, he,* etc.) and the relative pronoun *who,* are still fully inflected for the three cases:

Subjective (acting)   I, he, she, we, they, who

Possessive (possessing)   my (mine), your (yours), his, her (hers), its, our (ours), their (theirs), whose

Objective (acted upon)   me, him, her, us, them, whom

Center around   Illogical; use *center in* (or *on*) or *cluster around.*

Clause   A group of words containing a subject and a predicate. See **Independent clause** and **Dependent clause**.

Climactic, climatic   *Climactic* pertains to a climax; *climatic* pertains to climate.

Collective noun   A word identifying a class or a group of persons or things.

Comparative degree   In adjectives and adverbs, the comparative form made by adding *-er* or the word *more* (see **10a**).

Compare to, compare with   After *compare* when it shows similarity only, use *to;* in analyses of similarities and differences, use *with.*

She *compared* the wrecked train *to* strewn and broken matches.

She *compared* this train wreck *with* the one that occurred a month ago.

Complement   A word or group of words used to complete a predicate. Predicate adjectives, predicate nominatives, direct objects, and indirect objects are complements.

Complement, compliment   *To complement* means "to complete"; *to compliment* means "to praise."

Complex, compound sentences   A *complex sentence* has one independent clause and at least one dependent clause. A *compound sentence* has at least two independent clauses. A *compound-complex sentence* has at least two independent clauses and one dependent clause.

Compound subject   Two or more subjects connected by a coordinating conjunction such as *and* (see **7a**).

Conjunction   A word used to connect sentences or sentence parts. See also **Coordinating conjunction** and **Subordinating conjunction**.

49

Conjunctive adverb   An adverb used to relate two independent clauses separated by a semicolon in the same sentence or two independent clauses in adjoining sentences: *however, therefore, moreover, then, consequently, besides,* and so on (see **22a**).

Considerable   Basically an adjective, though used informally as a noun.

Standard   She had a *considerable* influence on her students.

Informal   He made *considerable* each week.

Contemptible, contemptuous   *Contemptible* means "deserving of scorn"; *contemptuous* means "feeling scorn."

The sophomore who was *contemptuous* toward freshmen was *contemptible.*

Continual, continuous   *Continual* refers to a prolonged and rapid succession; *continuous* refers to an uninterrupted succession.

Contraction   Avoid contractions *(don't, he's, they're)* in formal writing.

Coordinating conjunction   A simple conjunction which joins sentences and sentence parts of equal rank: *and, but, or, nor, for, yet, so.*

Correlative conjunction   A conjunction used as one of a pair to join coordinate sentence parts. The most common pairs are *either —or, neither —nor, not only —but also, both —and.*

Cute   Overused, many think, for such expressions as *pretty, dainty,* and *attractive.*

Data   Considered either singular or plural (see **7e**).

Deal   Informal and overused for *bargain, transaction,* or *business arrangement.* In *big deal,* slang.

Demonstrative adjective or pronoun   Word used to point out: *this, that, these, those.*

Dependent (subordinate) clause   A group of words which contains both a subject and a predicate but which does not stand alone as a sentence. A dependent clause is frequently signaled by a subordinator (*who, which, what, that, since, because,* and so on) and always functions as an adjective, adverb, or noun.

Adjective   The tenor *who sang the aria* had just arrived from Italy.

Noun   The critics agreed *that the young tenor had a magnificent voice.*

Adverb   *When he sang,* even the sophisticated audience was enraptured.

Differ from, differ with   *Differ from* expresses unlikeness; *differ with* expresses disagreement.

The twins *differ from* each other in personality.
The twins *differ with* each other about politics.

Direct address   The use of the name of a person or thing addressed directly.

Mary, have you seen the paper?

Direct object   A noun, pronoun, or other word receiving the action of the verb.

The angler finally caught the old *trout.*

Done   Past participle of *to do;* not to be used in place of *did,* as the past tense of *to do* (She *did* it, *not* She *done* it).

Don't   Contraction of *do not;* not to be used for *doesn't,* the contraction of *does not* (He *doesn't, not* He *don't*).

Double negative   Avoid such phrases as *can't do nothing, didn't have no, can't hardly,* and so on.

Effect See **Affect**.

Elliptical clause A clause in which one or more words are understood.

He admired no one else as much as *(he admired* or *he did)* her.

(understood markers pointing to "he admired" and "he did")

Enthused Use *enthusiastic* in formal writing.

Etc. Do not use *and etc.; etc.* means "and so forth." It should be set off by commas. *Etc.* is not considered appropriate in formal writing.

Ever, every Do not use *ever* for *every.* Use *every* in *every other, everybody, every now and then;* use *ever* in *ever so humble,* and so on.

Every day, everyday *Every day* is used as an adverb; *everyday,* as an adjective.

She comes to look at the same picture in the gallery *every day.*

Her trip to the gallery is an *everyday* occurrence.

Exam Informal. Use *examination* in formal writing.

Except See **Accept**.

Expect Informal for *believe, suspect, think, suppose,* and so forth.

Expletive A word such as *there* or *it* used in a sentence in which the subject follows the verb (see **7h**).

There are two people waiting outside.

Fabulous Informal for *extremely pleasing;* overused.

Fantastic Informal for *extraordinarily good;* overused.

Farther, further   Generally interchangeable, though many persons prefer *farther* in expressions of physical distance and *further* in expressions of time, quantity, and degree.

My car used less gasoline and went *farther* than hers.

The second speaker went *further* into the issues than the first.

Fewer, less   Use *fewer* to denote number; *less*, to denote amount or degree. *Fewer* refers to a plural word, *less* to a singular.

With *fewer* advertisers, there will be *less* income from advertising.

Fine   Often a poor substitute for a more exact word of approval or commendation.

Flunk   Informal. Prefer *fail* or *failure* in formal usage.

Folks   Informal for *family* or *relatives*.

Further   See **Farther**.

Gerund   See **Verbal**.

Good   Incorrect as an adverb. (She sings *well*, not She sings *good*).

Grand   Often vaguely used in place of more exact words like *majestic, magnificent, imposing.*

Great   Informal for *first-rate.*

Had, had of   Avoid *had of* for *had* (If I *had* seen you . . ., *not* If I *had of* seen you . . .).

Hang, hanged, hung   See page 9.

Hardly   See **Not hardly**.

Has got, have got   Use simply *has* or *have*.

Have, of   Avoid *could of, may of, might of, must of,* and *would of.* Use *could have, may have,* and so forth.

Himself See **Myself**.

Idiom A phrase with a unit meaning that cannot be suggested by the individual words. See **37d**.

Illusion See **Allusion**.

Imply, infer *Imply* means "to hint or suggest"; *infer* means "to draw a conclusion."

The speaker *implied* that Mr. Dixon was guilty.

The audience *inferred* that Mr. Dixon was guilty.

In, into *Into* denotes motion from the outside to the inside; *in* denotes position (enclosure).

The lion was *in* the cage when the trainer walked *into* the tent.

Indefinite pronoun A pronoun not pointing out a particular person or thing. Some of the most common indefinite pronouns are *some, any, each, every, everyone, somebody, anyone, anybody, one,* and *neither*.

Independent (main) clause A group of words which contains a subject and a predicate and which grammatically can stand alone as a sentence.

Indirect object A word which indirectly receives the action of the verb.

The singer wrote the *soldier* a letter.

Usually *to* or *for* is implied before the indirect object.

The singer wrote (to) the *soldier* a letter.

Infer See **Imply**.

Infinitive See **Verbal**.

In regards to Unidiomatic. Use *in regard to* or *with regard to*.

Intensive pronoun   A pronoun ending in *-self* and used for emphasis.

The director *himself* will act the part of Hamlet.

Interjection   A word used to exclaim or to express a strong emotion. It has no grammatical connections within its sentence. Some common interjections are *ah, oh,* and *ouch.*

Interrogative pronoun   A pronoun used in a question. *Who, whose, whom, what,* and *which* are interrogative pronouns.

Into   See **In.**

Intransitive verb   A verb that does not take an object.

Irregardless   Nonstandard for *regardless.*

Is when, is where   Ungrammatical use of an adverbial clause after a linking verb. Often misused in definitions and explanations.

Nonstandard   Combustion *is when* (or *is where*) oxygen unites with other elements.

Standard   Combustion occurs when oxygen unites with other elements.

Standard   Combustion is a union of oxygen with other elements.

Its, it's   *Its* is the possessive case of the pronoun *it; it's* is a contraction of *it is.*

It's exciting to parents when their baby cuts *its* first tooth.

Kind of, sort of   Informal as adverbs. Use *rather, somewhat,* and so forth.

Informal   Mr. Josephson was *sort of* disgusted.

Formal   Mr. Josephson was *rather* disgusted.

Formal   What *sort of* book is that? *(not an adverb)*

Kind of a, sort of a Delete the *a;* use *kind of* and *sort of.*

What *kind of* (not *kind of a*) car do you have?

Lay, lie See page 10.

Learn, teach *Learn* means "to acquire knowledge." *Teach* means "to impart knowledge."

He could not *learn* how to work the problem until Mrs. Smithers *taught* him the formula.

Less See **Fewer.**

Liable See **Likely.**

Lie See page 10.

Like Instead of *like* as a conjunction, prefer *as, as if,* or *as though.*

Conjunction She acted *like* she had never had a date before. (informal)

Conjunction She acted *as if* she had never been on the stage before. (standard)

Preposition She acted *like* a novice. (standard)

Such expressions as *tell it like it is* derive part of their appeal from their lighthearted defiance of convention.

Likely, liable Use *likely* to express probability; use *liable,* which may have legal connotations, to express responsibility.

You are *likely* to have an accident if you drive recklessly.
Since your father owns the car, he will be *liable* for damages.

Linking verb A verb which does not express action but links the subject to another word which names or describes it. Common linking verbs are *be, become,* and *seem.* See **10c.**

Loose A frequent misspelling of *lose. Loose* is usually an adjective; *lose* is a verb.

The performer wore a *loose* and trailing gown.

Speculators often *lose* their money.

Lot See **Alot**.

Lot of, lots of Informal in the sense of *much, many, a great deal.*

May See **Can**.

Modifier A word (or word group) which limits or describes another word. See **Adjective; Adverb**.

Mood The mood (or mode) of a verb indicates whether an action is to be thought of as fact, command, wish, or condition contrary to fact. Modern English has three moods: the indicative, for ordinary statements and questions; the imperative, for commands and entreaty; and the subjunctive, for certain idiomatic expressions of wish, command, or condition contrary to fact.

Indicative *Does* she play the guitar?
She *does.*

Imperative *Stay* with me.
Let him stay.
Let us pray.

Subjunctive If I *were* you, I would go.
I wish she *were* going with you.
I move that the meeting *be* adjourned.
It is necessary that he *stay* absolutely quiet.

The commonest subjunctive forms are *were* and *be.* All others are formed like the present-tense plural form, without -*s*.

Most Informal for *almost* in such expressions as the following.

> He is late for class *almost* (not *most*) every day.

Myself, yourself, himself, herself, itself These words are reflexives or intensives, not strict equivalents of *I, me, you, he, him, she, her, it.*

Intensive	I *myself* helped Father cut the wheat.
	I helped Father cut the wheat *myself.*
Reflexive	I cut *myself.*

Not	The elopement was known only to Sherry and *myself.*
But	The elopement was known only to Sherry and *me.*

Not	Only Kay and *myself* had access to the safe.
But	Only Kay and *I* had access to the safe.

Nice A weak substitute for more exact words like *attractive, modest, pleasant, kind,* and so forth.

Nominative case See **Case**.

Not hardly Double negative. Avoid; use *hardly.*

Noun A word which names. There are proper nouns, which name particular people, places, or things *(Thomas Jefferson, Paris,* the *Colosseum);* common nouns, which name one or more of a group *(alligator, high school, politician);* collective nouns (see **7d** and **8c**); abstract nouns, which name ideas, feelings, and beliefs *(religion, justice, dislike, enthusiasm);* concrete nouns, which name things perceived through the senses *(lemon, hatchet, worm).*

Noun clause See **Dependent clause.**

Nowheres Not considered standard; use *nowhere.*

Number See **Amount.**

Object of preposition See **Preposition** and **9b**.

Objective case See **Case**.

Obsolete word Not used in modern English. Examples: *jump* for "exactly" and *shrewd* in the sense of "bad" or "evil."

Of See **Have, of**.

Off of *Off* is sufficient.

He fell *off* (not *off of*) the water tower.

O.K., OK, okay Informal.

On a whole Confusion of two constructions, *as a whole* and *on the whole*.

Participle See **Verbal.**

Parts of speech The parts of speech are **Noun, Pronoun, Adjective, Verb, Adverb, Conjunction, Interjection, Preposition.** See each of these in this glossary.

Party Informal when used to mean *person,* except in legal usage.

Past participle The verb form used with an auxiliary, or helping, verb.

She had *won* the game.

Per cent, percent Use after figures, as "3 *per cent.*" Do not use for *percentage:*

Only a small *percentage* (not *per cent*) of the people had voted in the election.

Persecute, prosecute *Persecute* means "to oppress." *Prosecute* means "to take legal action against."

They were *persecuted* by hostile neighbors.
The district attorney will *prosecute* the driver of the car.

Personal pronoun A word like *I, you, he, she, it, we, they, mine, yours, his, hers, its, ours, theirs.*

Phenomena Plural; the singular is *phenomenon.*

Photo Informal.

Phrase A group of closely related words which do not contain both a subject and a predicate. There are subject phrases *(The new drill sergeant . . .),* verb phrases *(should have been),* verbal phrases *(climbing high mountains),* prepositional phrases *(in the living room),* appositive phrases (my brother, *the black sheep of the family),* and so forth.

Plenty Informal when used as an adverb.

Informal He was *plenty* sick.

Formal He was *very* sick.

P.M. *See* A.M.

Possessive case *See* **Case.**

Predicate The verb in a clause (simple predicate) or the verb and its modifiers and complements (complete predicate).

Predicate adjective An adjective following a linking verb and describing the subject (see **10c**).

The rose is *artificial.*

Predicate nominative *See* **Subjective complement.**

Predominate, predominant Do not use the verb *predominate* for the adjective *predominant.*

Preposition A connective which joins a noun or a pronoun to the rest of a sentence. A prepositional phrase may be used as either an adjective or an adverb.

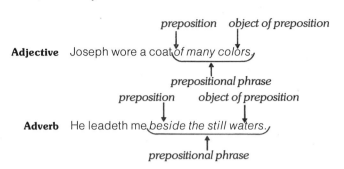

Adjective Joseph wore a coat of many colors.

preposition   object of preposition

prepositional phrase

Adverb He leadeth me beside the still waters.

preposition   object of preposition

prepositional phrase

Present participle See **Principal parts.**

Principal, principle Use *principal* to mean "the chief" or "most important." Use *principle* to mean "a rule" or "a truth."

The *principal* reason for her announcement was never discussed.

The *principal* of Brookwood High School resigned.

To act without *principle* leads to moral confusion.

Principal parts All verbs have three principal parts: the infinitive form *(to like),* the past tense *(liked),* and the past participle *(liked).* Sometimes the present participle *(liking)* is also considered a principal part. See **3.**

Pronominal adjective An adjective which is the possessive form of a pronoun (*my* book, *their* enthusiasm).

Pronoun A word which stands for a noun. See **Personal pronoun; Demonstrative adjective or pronoun; Reflexive pronoun; Intensive pronoun; Interrogative pronoun; Indefinite pronoun; Relative pronoun.**

Prosecute See **Persecute.**

Quote A verb. If a noun is required, use the word *quotation.*

Raise, rise See page 10.

Real Informal as an adverb meaning "really" or "very."

Reason is (was) because Especially in writing, do not use for *the reason is that. Because* should introduce an adverbial clause, not a noun clause used as a subjective complement.

Not The *reason* Abernathy enlisted *was because* he could not find a job.

But The *reason* Abernathy enlisted *was that* he could not find a job.

Or Abernathy enlisted *because* he could not find a job.

Reflexive pronoun A pronoun ending in *-self* and indicating that the subject acts upon itself. See **Myself.**

The butcher cut *himself.*

Relative pronoun A pronoun used to introduce a dependent clause. Relative pronouns are *who, whose, whom, what, which, that,* and the forms with *-ever.*

Respectfully, respectively *Respectfully* means "with respect"; *respectively* means "each in the order given."

She *respectfully* thanked the principal for her diploma.

Crossing the platform, she passed by the speaker, the superintendent, and the valedictorian *respectively.*

Revelant A misspelling and mispronunciation of *relevant.*

Said Not to be used in the sense of *previously mentioned,* except in legal style (The *said* object was found in the room of the accused).

Same Rarely used as a pronoun unless it is preceded by *the,* except in legal style (Drinking by minors is illegal and *same* shall result in arrest).

Sensual, sensuous *Sensual* connotes gratification of the physical senses; *sensuous* refers to what is experienced through the senses, often connoting the enjoyment of beauty.

Set, sit   *See* page 10.

Shall, will   In strictly formal English, to indicate simple futurity, *shall* is conventional in the first person (I *shall, we shall*); *will,* in the second and third persons (you *will,* he or she *will,* they *will*). To indicate determination, duty, or necessity, *will* is formal in the first person (I *will, we will*); *shall,* in the second and third persons (you *shall,* he or she *shall,* they *shall*). These distinctions are weaker than they used to be, and *will* is increasingly used in all persons.

Shape up   Informal for "to develop satisfactorily."

Simple sentence   A sentence consisting of only one independent clause and no dependent clauses.

So   For the use of *so* in incomplete constructions, see **13a.** The use of *so* for *so that* sometimes causes confusion, as in the following example.

Not Clear   She came here *so* she could see all the family. (Result or purpose?)

    Clear   She came here *so that* she could see all the family. (Purpose)

Sometime, some time   *Sometime* is used adverbially to designate an indefinite point of time. *Some time* refers to a period or duration of time.

I will see you *sometime* next week.

I have not seen her for *some time.*

Sort of   *See* **Kind of.**

Sort of a   *See* **Kind of a.**

Subject   A word or group of words about which the sentence or clause makes a statement.

    Simple Subject   *Whitman* left the lecture on astronomy.

Compound Subject *Whitman* and *Emerson* were nineteenth-century writers.

Clause as Subject *That Whitman left the lecture on astronomy* is well known.

Subjective case See **Case**.

Subjective complement A word or group of words which follows a linking verb and identifies the subject.

This book is a best-selling historical *novel.*

His excuse was *that he had been sick.*

Subjunctive See **Mood**.

Subordinate clause See **Dependent clause**.

Subordinating conjunction A conjunction which joins sentence parts of unequal rank. Most frequently it begins a dependent clause. Some common subordinating conjunctions are *because, since, though, although, if, when, while, before, after, as, until, so that, as long as, as if, where, unless, as soon as, whereas, in order that.*

Superlative degree In adjectives and adverbs, the superlative form made by adding -*est* or the word *most* (see **10a**).

Sure Informal as an adverb for *surely, certainly.*

Informal The speaker *sure* criticized her opponent.

Formal The speaker *certainly* criticized her opponent.

Sure and, try and Use *sure to, try to.*

Be *sure to* (not *sure and*) notice the costumes of the dancers.

Suspicion Avoid as a verb. Use *suspect.*

Take See **Bring**.

Teach See **Learn**.

Tense   The time of the action expressed by a verb: past, present, or future. See **4.**

Terrible   Often a poor substitute for a more exact word.

Than, then   Do not misspell one of these words and use it for the other.

Harriet is taller *than* Irene.

Then Doris spoke to the group.

Their, there   Not interchangeable: *their* is the possessive of *they; there* is either an adverb meaning "in that place" or an expletive.

Their dachshund is sick.

There is a veterinarian's office in this block. (Expletive)

There it is on the corner. (Adverb of place)

These (those) kind, these (those) sort   *These (those)* is plural; *kind (sort)* is singular. Therefore use *this (that) kind, this (that) sort; these (those) kinds, these (those) sorts.*

This here, that there   Omit *here* and *there;* they are not needed.

Not   *That there* is my house.

But   *That* is my house.

Thusly   *Thus* is preferable.

Transitive verb   A verb that may take an object.

Try and   See **Sure and.**

Unique   Means "one of a kind"; hence it may not logically be compared. *Unique* should not be loosely used for *unusual* or *remarkable.*

Use   Sometimes carelessly written for the past tense, *used.*

Thomas Jefferson *used* (not *use*) to bathe in cold water.

Verb   A word or group of words expressing action, being, or state of being.

What *is* life?
The fire *has been built.*

Verbal   A word derived from a verb and used as a noun, an adjective, or an adverb. A verbal may be a gerund, a participle, or an infinitive.

Gerund   1. ends in *-ing*
2. is used as a noun

gerund   *object of gerund*

Shoeing horses is almost a lost art.

gerund phrase, used as subject

Participle   1. usually ends in *-ing, -ed,* or *-d*
2. is used as an adjective

prepositional phrase, modifying participle

participle

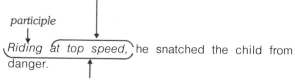

Riding at top speed, he snatched the child from danger.

participial phrase, modifying subject

Infinitive   1. begins with *to,* which may be understood
2. is used as an adjective, an adverb, or a noun

infinitive   *object of infinitive*

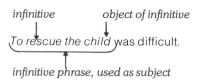

To rescue the child was difficult.

infinitive phrase, used as subject

infinitive, used as adjective

Charlotte's Web is a good book *to read* to a child.

infinitive, used as adverb

He was eager *to ride* his new horse.

Verb phrase   *See* **Phrase.**

Voice   Transitive verbs have two forms to show whether their subjects act (active voice) or are acted upon (passive voice). See page 15.

Wait on   Unidiomatic for *wait for. Wait on* correctly means "to serve."

Ways   Prefer *way* when designating a distance (a long *way, not* a long *ways*).

When, where   *See* **Is when, is where.**

Where   Do not misuse for *that.*

I read in the newspaper *that* (not *where*) you saved a child's life.

Where at   The *at* is unnecessary.

Not   *Where* is he *at?*

But   *Where* is he?

Who, whom   *See* **9i.**

Whose, who's   *Whose* is the possessive of *who; who's* is a contraction of *who is.*

-wise   A suffix overused in combinations with nouns, such as *budgetwise, progresswise,* and *businesswise.*

Without   Dialectal for *unless,* as in "I cannot come *without* you pay for the ticket."

Index

Q